Cinematic Political Thought

Taking on the Political
Series Editors: Benjamin Arditi and Jeremy Valentine
International Advisory Editors: Jane Bennet, Michael Dillon
and Michael J. Shapiro

The purpose of the series *Taking on the Political* is to provide a space of engagement with the expanded field of the political that continues to inspire and provoke critical inquiry and practical invtervention. hence the colloquial sense of *taking on* as both accepting and challenging the policital – the predicament in which one is located in the absence of an extra-political foundation. The series will publish works that address this predicament through such themes as ethical responsibility and commonality, emerging strategies of goverance, subjectivity and power, the legacies of political modernity and the political dimension of postfoundational thought. In addition to engaging with these themes the series is particularly interested in taking on the conventions through which they are expressed.

Cinematic Political Thought

Narrating Race, Nation and Gender

Michael J. Shapiro

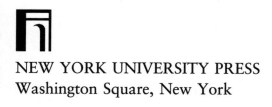

NEW YORK UNIVERSITY PRESS
Washington Square, New York

First published in the U.S.A. in 1999 by
NEW YORK UNIVERSITY PRESS
Washington Square
New York, NY 10003

CIP data available from the Library of Congress
ISBN 0-8147-9750-4 (cloth)
ISBN 0-8147-9751-2 (paperback)

Typeset in 11 on 13 Sabon
by Hewer Text Ltd, Edinburgh, and
printed and bound in Great Britain by
MPG Books Ltd, Bodmin

Contents

For Hannah: again and always

Acknowledgements

I am indebted to the series editors, Benjamin Arditi, Mick Dillon, and Jeremy Valentine for extensive comments on earlier drafts of the manuscript as a whole and to Tom Dumm, Larry George, Jane Bennett, Dale Bauer, William Connolly, Miriam Cooke, Jorge Fernandez, Kate Manzo, Hannah Tavares, and Rob Walker for critical responses to individual chapters.

Introduction

This book is both a series of investigations into aspects of contemporary politics and a more general attempt to articulate a critical philosophical perspective with politically disposed treatments of contemporary cinema. The aim is to engage in political thought without closing the question of 'the political'. What I offer is a politics of critique, which, in a Kantian spirit, specifies an attitude rather than a particular destination. My investigations treat various aspects of the present, but they are anti-diegetic and non-hermeneutic; I attribute no clear historical direction to the temporal differences with which I deal and I do not seek to attract a particular interpretation of contemporary life-worlds. This is a polemical work, aimed at encouraging critical, ethico-political thinking, not at deepening an understanding of what are generally taken as the spaces of the political. It is polemical not in the sense – disparaged by Foucault – of being accusatory rather than dialogic[1] but in the sense – encouraged by Deleuze and Guattari – of treating concepts as normative and political rather than merely cognitive.[2] It is also polemical in the sense suggested in Carl Schmitt's claim that 'all political concepts, images, and terms have polemical meaning'[3] inasmuch as my analyses are not aimed at developing a set of generalized abstractions but are 'focused on specific conflict[s] and are bound to . . . concrete situation[s]'.[4]

Because my treatment of the politics of critique is indebted to a critical legacy initiated in the philosophical texts of Immanuel Kant, his writings are summoned at various junctures in my investigations. My engagement with Kant does not result in exegesis; rather than situating my analysis in the history of contention over how Kant's texts ought to be understood, I stage critical encounters with his philosophical imaginary and his constructions of global space. But despite my departures from many of his philosophical and ethico-political positions, Kant's project of critique inspires my attempt to provide a critical intervention into aspects of contemporary politics, to exemplify what it can mean to *think* the political.

Although the point is controversial, I assume that Kant's contribution to creating a philosophical subject, which continues to orient much of contemporary philosophical thinking, is heavily politically inflected. Doubtless, reflecting the historical influences on his writing – his three major works on critique straddle the events of the French Revolution, and his reflections on the possibility of an enduring global peace explicitly engage the events in France – Kant's approach to the 'what is man' query he raises is doubtless affected by the historical influences on his writing. Given his reflections on the significance of the French Revolution and his disposition against both religious and political structures of domination, Kant constructed personhood not only as a priori structures of apprehension but also as a judging intellect that emerges in a political milieu. Kant's human subjects are cognizing moral citizens who are meant to displace the passive subjects of both monarchs and church hierarchies. His philosophical subject is therefore philosophico-political or, to use Balibar's discerning contraction, 'cosmopolitical'.[5]

Kant's political subject is introduced to do more, however, than oppose religious and monarchical authority within the state. His citizen-subject contains a disposition extending beyond national borders; it is a global citizen, whose capacity for edification on the basis of publicity about political events, disposes her or him away from a narrow nationalist partisanship and towards a cosmopolitan hospitality. For this reason, Kant's political ideas continue to influence perspectives – mine included – that seek to oppose commitments to a narrow identity politics at a national level and security-mindedness at the level of global political exchange.

Kant's philosophical politics also attracts me because of its affirmation of contingency. Although he strove to anchor the thinking of his political subject in universalities, Kant introduced a model of thought that escapes the authority of a fixed subjectivity enthralled by a world of things-in-themselves. And, even as he strove to invent a transcendental subject, bent on achieving a unity of experience, the conflict he staged between the demands of reason and the work of imagination introduces a centrifugal element that works against the more pacifying tropes he employed to harmonize subjective faculties.[6] As a result he has inspired the critical thinking of such contemporary theorists as Deleuze, Derrida, Foucault, and Lyotard, whom I am loosely regarding as post-Kantians. They acquire the prefix, 'post', because while they identify with Kant's line of escape from empiricist and hermeneutic models of epistemic closure, they resist his tendency to contain the radical openness and contingency that his model of critique proposes within homogenizing conceptions of individual and collective subjects.

Similarly, while much of my thinking is indebted to Kant's politically invested philosophical work and his critical rejection of closural models of interpretation – his recognition that thought is productive rather than merely representational – I have found it necessary, nevertheless, to resist aspects of Kant's political imaginary and his location of critical thought strictly within the domain of mental faculties. Kant left an ambiguous legacy. On the one hand, he recognized that some concepts, those that operate within the speculative imagination, have unstable boundaries, but, on the other, his desire for stable boundaries in both the geo-political world of states and in the philosophical world of concepts had him shrinking from an exploration of the domains of the unthought that his philosophy had rendered accessible.

Philosophically, Kant narrowed his model of thinking to the domain of mental faculties. He contained difference by locating the movement of thought within a narrative that begins with raw experience, is followed by productive understanding, and then, under the influence of publicity, yields a universal common sense. Politically, Kant narrowed his vision to the space of governmental states, even though he urged a tolerant attitude towards those who traverse state boundaries. Just as in his philosophical world, he sought a movement of thought that would reduce contingency rather than embracing it, in his thoroughly statist political world, he sought a universalism rather than recognizing the extent to which any political code will necessarily produce an outside within (in Foucault's terms) or an uncoded, enigmatic nomadism moving in smooth spaces that states have failed to subdue and overcode (in Deleuze and Guattari's).

Despite his major role in inventing the conditions of possibility for critical thought, then, Kant helped to inaugurate a philosophical discourse that, despite its cosmopolitan aspirations, is thoroughly statist. Deleuze and Guattari have (hyperbolically) summarized this Kantian complicity with state power:

> Ever since philosophy assigned itself the role of ground it has been giving established powers its blessing, and tracing its doctrine of faculties onto

the organs of state power. Common sense, the unity of the faculties at the center constituted by the Cogito, is the state consensus raised to the level of the absolute.[7]

Although Deleuze and Guattari's statement here tends towards an exaggerated anti-Kantianism, belied by their dependence on his legacy, their general point is important: to discern connections between philosophical imaginaries and political positions, it is necessary to resist the idea that philosophical discourse stands outside of an engagement with practical domains of political relations. Accordingly, their conceptual practice manifests a countertendency to that characteristic of philosophers who imagine that philosophy convokes a master discourse, those who think of philosophy as a practice of thought capable of investigating the value of other discourses from a dispassionate and non-partisan epistemological space.

Hegel, for example, an exemplar of this tendency, radically divorced philosophical thought from popular thought, political and otherwise, in his introduction to his philosophy of history. And Hegel had simply inherited a venerable position. As Michele Le Doeuff has put it: 'It is indeed a very old commonplace to associate philosophy with a certain *logos* thought of as defining itself through opposition to other types of discourse.'[8] Increasingly of late, however, critical thinkers in philosophy and the humanities have reminded us that philosophy is, among other things, a historically situated literature. Like other modes of discourse, its rhetorical motions are closely tied to models of the world in general and to the practice of philosophy as it was specifically deployed in lifeworlds in particular during philosophy's various moments of gestation and elaboration.

Jacques Derrida has noted, for example, that the history of philosophy is a history of obliteration. Its founding, sensuous tropes have been erased; they are invisible within the more abstract, metaphysical expressions that appear as articulations from which experiential figures have been largely evacuated.[9] A genealogical approach to philosophy, one that recovers the conditions of emergence of its idioms, can recover much of the invisible ink to which Derrida refers in his exegesis of philosophy's obliterational history. For example, philosophy for the ancient Greeks was not only a practice of argumentation but also a practice of thought designed to cure the soul, to bring peace and comfort, given the recognition that life includes morbidity and death. For centuries, Christian thought incorporated this latter aspect of Greek philosophy, re-inflecting it to comport with the Christian practice of meditation and spirituality, but maintaining, at the same time, the health-oriented tropes that structured the concepts of life and well being in the Greek world. Thus the writings of St.'s Augustine and Ambrose are replete with figures related to the arts of healing that structured much of Greek philosophical thought.

One need not go back, however, to late antiquity's Christian writers to witness the contagion of the tropes vehiculating the Greek philosophical imaginary. Kant, figured the cognitive faculty in terms of its health versus illness and saw philosophy as, among other things, a health-enabling regime of thought, a goad to stimulate those who would sink into the morbidity of inactivity, from which 'death would follow inevitably,'[10] and a 'heroic medicine' with which to fight 'political evils' with effective 'prophetic intervention.'[11]

Pierre Hadot, a historian of ancient thought, has discerned the legacy of the Greek art of healing in contemporary philosophy as well, specifically in Ludwig Wittgenstein's philosophical imaginary:

> It is a therapeutics that is offered to us. Philosophy is an illness of language . . . The true philosophy will therefore consist in curing itself of philosophy, in making every philosophical problem completely and definitively disappear . . . Wittgenstein continues [from the *Tractatus* to the *Investigations*] . . . to devote himself to the same mission: to bring a radical and definitive peace to metaphysical worry.[12]

Walter Benjamin expressed agreement with these sentiments, using the same health-oriented tropes. In his criticism of Kantian metaphysics, he remarked, 'In epistemology every metaphysical element is the germ of a disease that expresses itself in the separation of knowledge from the realm of experience in its full freedom and depth.'[13]

While much can be said about the influence of ancient philosophical idioms that remain present in contemporary philosophical imaginaries, I want to focus again on Kant, whose ambiguous legacy Benjamin well recognized.[14] Despite his oft-expressed allergy to metaphor, Kant's philosophical discourse was, in various ways, also a figuratively enhanced, political polemic. At the same time that his invention of critique was aimed at disclosing the conditions of possibility for a critical *reading* of an emerging modernity, he was constructing the philosophical author as one who should not only encourage a healthy level of intellectual activity but also help nudge humanity into a more hospitable and just political direction. The Kantian philosophical writer does not merely read the signs of the times; he or she is a historical *actor*, seeking to help bring about the favourable political ends that philosophical prognostication discerns.[15]

The details of my ambivalent relationship to Kant emerge in the chapters that follow. Here, I want to note that my critical interventions into contemporary political issues, indebted as they are to a Kantian politics of critique, take a post-Kantian turn, influenced especially by two Nietzsche-inspired ways of situating the radical contingency of the present. The first is a Foucauldian mode of genealogical history and the second a Deleuzian mode of cinematic thinking. Both of these modes of thinking are described as they are applied in Chapter 1. What I want to note in addition is that much of the critical aspect of my thinking is deployed in two different ways in which modern cinema figures in my investigations.

First, in each chapter I analyze films that exemplify aspects of my arguments. Second, I attempt to structure much of my writing cinematically. Walter Benjamin made a similar point about the cinematic influences on the writing style one needs to render history politically.[16] He identified the writing vehicle of his arcades project as 'literary montage,' suggesting that rather than what he says, it is what he 'exhibits' (*zeigen*)[17]; the juxtapositions of various images he provides render the 'time of the now'[18] from a critical, historically sensitive perspective.

Benjamin's brief remarks, in which he figures his writing in cinematic language, are epigrammatic rather than programmatic. Gilles Deleuze's extensive analysis of the movement and time images of modern cinema provides a more sustained inspiration for my attempt to approach cinematic style in some of my writing. By directing a series of engagements and juxtapositions among different thought models and different historical moments, I seek to make the present surprising and contingent rather than simply a refinement of certain widely accepted chronologies of historical political trends.[19] In addition to engaging in critical interventions that make use of genealogical and deconstructive modes of interpretation (among others), I make use of the radical temporality of cinematic composition, which, by its mode of presentation, resists the perspectives of the characters and groups whose actions it portrays. Through its cuts, juxtapositions, and the temporal trajectories of its images, cinematic writing-as-critical-thought assembles an alternative perspective to those narrations that support the coherences of bounded individual and collective identities.

But the politics of critique I develop, as I map and compose various domains of political contention, is not aimed at merely disrupting the presently constituted modes of authority and power that inhere in the identity- and security-oriented stories and discourses of the present. Critique, in the post-Kantian sense in which I am using it, is ethical as well as political.[20] In my various explorations of domains of political exclusion, for example, modes of identity and security politics that reject various forms of movement, both substantive (for example, immigration flows of the 1990s) and symbolic (such as migrating sexualities), I seek to encourage a hospitality towards ambiguous, protean and unsettled modes of selfhood and community. Such a hospitality, which I address in Chapter 3 explicitly, extends recognition not simply to given types of people but to the possibilities of personhood and interpersonal engagement that exist but remain unrecognized within institutionalized and administered understandings. My treatment of these aspects of the unthought or the virtual within the actual begins in Chapter 1 with an analysis of what, after Walter Benjamin's felicitous phrasing, I term the politics of 'now-time'.

Notes

1. Foucault states that a polemic 'isn't dealing with an interlocutor, it is processing a suspect': Michel Foucault, 'Polemics, Politics and Problematizations: An Interview', in Paul Rabinow (ed.) *The Foucault Reader* (New York: Pantheon, 1984), p. 382.
2. See Gilles Deleuze and Félix Guattari, *What is Philosophy?*, trans. Hugh Tomlinson and Graham Burchell (New York: Columbia University Press, 1994).
3. Carl Schmitt, *The Concept of the Political*, trans. George Schwab (New Brunswick, NJ.: Rutgers University Press, 1976), p. 30.
4. Ibid.
5. Étienne Balibar, 'Subjection and Subjectivation', in Joan Copjek (ed.), *Supposing the Subject* (London: Verso, 1994), p. 6.
6. See in particular Section no. 27 of Immanuel Kant, *The Critique of Judgement*, trans. James Creed Meredith (New York: Oxford University Press, 1952).

7. Gilles Deleuze and Félix Guattari, *A Thousand Plateaus*, trans. Brian Massumi (Minneapolis: University of Minnesota Press, 1987), p. 376.

8. Michele Le Doeuff, *The Philosophical Imaginary*, trans. Colin Gordon (London: Athlone, 1989). p. 1.

9. Jacques Derrida, 'White Mythologies', in *Margins of Philosophy*, trans. Alan Bass (Chicago: University of Chicago Press, 1982), p. 213.

10. Immanuel Kant, *Anthropology from a Pragmatic Point of View*, trans. Victor Lyle Dowdell (Carbondale: Southern Illinois University Press), p. 136. A good discussion of the health metaphors in Kant's philosophy is in Jean-François Lyotard, 'Judiciousness in Dispute, or Kant after Marx', trans. Cecile Lindsay in Andrew Benjamin (ed.), *The Lyotard Reader* (Cambridge: Basil Blackwell, 1989), pp. 324–59.

11. Immanuel Kant, 'The Contest of Faculties', in Hans Reiss, ed. Andrew Benjamin (ed.), *The Lytoaid Political Writings* (New York: Cambridge University Press, 1991), p. 189–90.

12. Pierre Hadot, quoted in Arnold I. Davidson's 'Introduction' to Hadot's *Philosophy as a Way of life*, trans. Michael Chase (London: Blackwell, 1995), p. 17.

13. Walter Benjamin, 'On the Program of the Coming Philosophy', trans. Mark Ritter, in Gary Smith (ed.), *Benjamin: Philosophy, History, Aesthetics* (Chicago: University of Chicago Press, 1989), p. 3.

14. See Ibid., pp. 1–12.

15. Kant makes this argument in both 'Perpetual Peace' and 'The Contest of Faculties'.

16. Benjamin's specific reference to *Jetztzeit* is in 'Theses on the Philosophy of History', in *Illuminations*, trans. Harry Zohn (New York: Schocken, 1969), p. 261.

17. Walter Benjamin, 'N [Re The Theory of Knowledge, Theory of Progress]', trans. Leigh Hafrey and Richard Sieburth, in Smith (ed.), *Benjamin: Philosophy, History, Aesthetics*, p. 47.

18. Benjamin, 'Theses on the Philosophy of History', p. 263.

19. Deleuze's remarks about the cinema author are apropos here. Inspired by Kafka's role as a literary author, Deleuze's cinema author 'finds himself before a people which, from the point of view of culture, are doubly colonized: colonized by stories that have come from elsewhere, but also by their own myths become personal entities at the service of the colonizer'. Gilles Deleuze,

Cinema 2, trans. Hugh Tomlinson and Robert Galeta (London: Athlone, 1989), p. 222.

20. Foucault argues this point in 'What is Critique?', trans. Lysa Hochroth in Michel Foucault, *The Politics of Truth*, Sylvere Lotringer and Lysa Hochroth (eds), (New York: Semiotext(e), 1997), pp. 23–82.

1

Towards a Politics of Now-Time: Reading *Hoop Dreams* with Kubrick's *Barry Lyndon*

Introduction: Ray Agnew's Interception

On Monday, October 28 1996, sports journalist Mike Freeman's report on the Sunday Giants–Lions game, in the *New York Times*, featured a pass interception by the Giants' Ray Agnew:

> This is an image that might endure in the minds of the Lions for months to come: Giants defensive lineman Ray Agnew, after picking off a pass, rumbling 34 yards for a touchdown, his 285 pound body running so slowly it seemed the feat couldn't be captured on an hour long highlight show.[1]

If the phenomenon of professional football is confined to the playing field, the value of Ray Agnew's performance was 6 points, added to the Giants' score. But it is clear to Freeman that the spatio-temporality of contemporary sports exceeds what occurs during playing time. In extending the temporal boundaries of the Agnew event into a post-game media future, Freeman offers, in a remarkably efficient sentence, a sophisticated reading of how sports are now experienced. He recognizes that the value of Agnew's interception is also contingent on its duration. To be re-experienced as publicity, it must fit within an hour-long episode of sports television, at the end of the day.

To achieve a critical perspective on the ethico-political significance of the Agnew event, I want to locate Freeman's insights in a broader field of events and to take note of Agnew's identity as a black athlete. The purposes of this extension are both simple and complex. At a simple level, the aim is to analyze the contemporary experience of sports. At a more complex level, the aim is to explore critically the time-value relationships of the present, with particular reference to how these relationships are articulated in the movement and containment of black bodies. The first aim requires an understanding of the genealogy of sports, which is briefly sketched below. The second, to which I turn immediately, requires a sorting through of philosophies of the event, with an eye towards a propitious way to characterize what Walter Benjamin called now–time (*Jetztzeit*).[2] To locate Ray Agnew's performance as an event in now-time, we must capture the event conceptually and critically; we must think it in a way that illuminates the present from an uncommon perspective and, in accord with Benjamin's political sensibility, treat the politics of the present in a way that affords a politically perspicuous, historical view of the past as well.[3] Having evoked the idea of the critical (for the second time) as well as challenging the notion of common sense, it is time to summon Immanuel Kant.

Enlisting/Resisting Kant

Why turn to Kant, who was among other things a philosopher of common sense, when what is sought is an uncommon sense? Although I will argue that Kant's commitment to a universalistic model of thought is ultimately disenabling for thinking the present, I want to argue as well that it is Kant who also creates the conditions of possibility for an uncommon, critical encounter with the present. Kant addressed the relevant question. He asked not only about the certainty of knowledge but also, as Benjamin aptly put it, about 'the integrity of an experience that is ephemeral'.[4]

In his approach to that question – to put it simply at the outset – Kant impeached the empiricist narrative of experience which privileges objects. Denying that things in themselves can command the structure of experience, Kant offered a narrative of understanding in which a representing faculty is implicated in the constitution of phenomena. And, most significantly for treating the event in question, that faculty, in the form of a shaping, productive understanding, constitutes phenomena with a sensibility that involves 'relations of time'.[5]

To treat the issue more extensively, I want to note the ways in which Kant's philosophy of experience inaugurates a critical view of the kind of exemplary experience that Freeman describes. At a general level, Kantian critique is aimed at asking how it is that an intelligible experience is possible, given our lack of access to things in themselves. His answer mobilizes various metaphors to treat, ultimately, the role of the faculty of judgement in his third, and consummating, critique. His most persistent figuration is governmental: he suggests that the achievement of intelligibility requires an integration of the various faculties through which phenomena are constituted, with judgement as the mediating mechanism, providing the 'transitions' among the various domains over which the different faculties exercise their respective legislative authorities.[6]

At a philosophical level, the Kantian construction of experience is critical, both because it recognizes that the raw matter involved in the flow of events does not by itself add up to a meaningful experience – what is required is what Kant calls a subject engaged in a 'representational activity'[7] – and because that representational activity does not achieve a natural closure.[8] The (non-closural) narrative structure of the Kantian account of experience (presented most comprehensively in his Third Critique, but also developed elsewhere, especially in his Anthropology) is as follows: first there is 'organic sensation;'[9] but because sensation generates a disordered set of disparate perceptions, the cognitive faculty then becomes activated to order them. Sense perception is prior to an integrated understanding: 'sense perceptions certainly precede perceptions of the understanding'[10]; it is the stage in which the subject is merely affected by the world. However, it is followed by 'understanding' as the cognitive faculty 'joins perceptions and combines them under a rule of thought by introducing order into the manifold'.[11]

But this active aspect of perception, Kant's productive understanding, has not finished its task until it universalizes itself and goes public. Going public, however, is not a process of social communication. This portion of the narrative of experience is what Kant designates as enlightenment at the level of the subject, whose consciousness is engaged in reflection. The judging faculty of taste contains – on reflection – the assumption of a 'universal voice' that, at the stage of mere reflection, is an 'idea' whose confirmation must be postponed.[12] Finally, because that same reflecting faculty contains a prior estimate of its universal communicability,[13] the movement of reflective consciousness gives rise to the public sphere (in a strictly formal sense) in that what begins with matter and is then given form ultimately becomes common or social. The ultimate part of the narrative is the movement to what Kant calls a 'universal communicability', which, he says, is something that 'everyone expects and requires from everyone else'.[14]

The enlightenment achieved in this narrative is a process by which the subject, as a form of reflective consciousness, becomes larger than experience. Kant's solution to the aporias of experience is to make the subject larger than the world. This enlargement is effected by letting go of the sensible world: the subject's experience realizes its universality and communicability, Kant states, by virtue of the subject's 'letting go the element of matter'[15] and thereby accomplishing '*enlarged* thought'.[16] The narrative of experience is a story of judgement moving the subject towards a *sensus communis* 'without the mediation of a concept'[17] and without actual social communication. The expansion does not involve communicative dissemination. What increases is the size and coherence of the subject's comprehension.

We have to look elsewhere in Kant's writings to discover social as opposed to cognitive expansion. The social analogue to the individual enlightenment narrative can be found in Kant's political writings. Kant's hoped-for global enlightenment is a process that is structurally homologous with the process of enlargement he attributes to the enlightened subject. Just as the individual process of enlightenment aims, through the exercise of the faculty of judgement, to produce a harmony among the various spheres of the intellect and thereby achieve experience that is common and universally communicable, the publicity achieved by important events must lead to a globally shared experience and ultimately a moral *sensus communis*, embodying a global harmony. People everywhere, reading the 'signs of the times' would move, Kant hoped, towards a universal, cosmopolitan tolerance:

> The peoples of the earth . . . have entered in varying degrees into a universal community, and it has developed to the point where a violation of rights in *one* part of the world is felt *everywhere*.[18]

Kant's reading of the 'signs of the times' was inflected by both a current event, the French Revolution, and a more general, teleological commitment about the historical tendency of humanity: his prognostication that it was moving towards a more peaceful epoch. To discern a moral purpose in history, he thought, it is necessary to read historical signs, in particular to search for an important event which would allow us to conclude that 'mankind is improving'.[19]

Kantian temporality is thus divided into two structurally isomorphic enlightenment stories, one at the level of the subject and one at the level of international society. To what extent, we can now ask, does the Kantian story of experience, at both levels, fit the event in question? Certainly Ray Agnew's event, both the on-field performance and its futurity as a highlight on sports television, is public. And the temporality of experiencing the event more or less fits the Kantian enlightenment narrative. There is the raw experience – a large body in motion – then there is the imposition of form on the experience, resulting in a score that is calculated in a way that integrates it within prescribed concepts; and, finally, because it involves a performance whose singularity stands out, it becomes (barely) appropriate for summarizing the action in subsequent publicity. It is featured on televisual and printed media with almost global distribution.

Just as certainly, however, Kant's mental formalism – his story of the individual subject's enlightenment through enlargement, which characterizes the later stages of the event – is inadequate for treating the way the event achieves meaning and value, commonly or un-commonly. And his model of enlightenment at the social level hardly allows us to appreciate how the description of the event can produce a critical reading of the present.

Leaving aside, for the moment, the uncommon sense needed to capture the event in terms of political insight – by which I mean the sense in which one can recognize what is special about today as opposed to yesterday with respect to the control implications of the spatio-temporality of sports – the Kantian reliance on cognitive faculties and his construction of the public sphere based on a shared mentality fail to illuminate the event's peculiarly contemporary in-telligibility. 'We' (sports fans) know what Mike Freeman means; we can share his coding of the event-as-experience, not because of a shared structure of apprehension, in which time is internal to our subjectivity, but because current *practices* of temporality govern the event. Such practices shape the organization of sports, of media, and of our structures of sociality in general. To the extent that we experience an event together as the same kind of event – and there are certainly diverse interpretive communities – we do so because of the way a complex set of spatio-temporal practices, which constitute 'now-time,' shape the event and its reception as such. And the more social dimension of Kant's model of enlightenment, his conception of the effects of reading the signs of the times, cannot render the event in critical political terms because the reading of events is mediated by structures and technologies of dissemination, not merely by perceiving faculties, made coherent by the exercise of judgement.

Nevertheless, while Kant's notion of the *sensus communis* is ulti-mately cognitive and formal rather than social and cultural, failing to provide a discernment of the complex process by which experiences are encoded in general and how they are re-inflected critically by those who seek to render them from different angles of vision, his introduction of a critical attitude towards modernity remains instructive. He provides an avenue for understanding the way the value of Ray Agnew's performance can be located in a more critical horizon of contemporary values.

Two contemporary thinkers, Michel Foucault and Gilles Deleuze, both edified by Kant's contribution to critique, provide thought vehicles for this purpose. In the case of Foucault, the vehicle is a genealogical approach to the events of the present. In the case of Deleuze, the vehicle is a demonstration of the way contemporary cinema provides a mode of thought about time and events that encodes the peculiarities of the present. Both Foucault and Deleuze resist Kant's conception of a universalistic, legislative power inherent in the common sense of mental faculties. Influenced by Nietzsche's attack on a philosophical tradition – exemplified by Kant – that has created a mode of thinking able only 'to take everything that has hitherto happened and been valued, and make it clear, distinct, intelligible and manageable',[20] Foucault and Deleuze employ conceptual strategies that resist institutionalized forms of intelligibility. Access to an uncommon sense, Nietzsche insisted, comes through a different kind of legislation, a law-giving that inheres in creative conceptual effort. Foucault's and Deleuze's glosses on Kant, and their Nietzsche-inspired re-inflections, follow.

The Foucauldian Gloss

As is evident in Kant's political writings, his philosophical search for a universalistic basis for experience was accompanied by a more specific set of commentaries on the events of his day. While Kant strove to pose the 'who' question, the question about the human subject writ large, at the level of the philosophy of experience, at the level of social commentary, he deployed his approach to value and judgement on his own historical period, seeking a politically perspicuous understanding of his time. With one mind he constructed a universalistic, timeless narrative, with another, he resisted that universalistic narrative and operated at the level of the historical example.[21]

Kant's attention to his own historical time is especially evident in his text on enlightenment, where, as Foucault suggests, 'he is not seeking to understand the present on the basis of a totality or of a future achievement. He is looking for difference: What difference does today introduce with respect to yesterday.'[22] Instead of prescribing a trans-cendental attitude towards value, which encourages us to ask *what* it is, given how subjects can, in a universalistic sense, make experience coherent, Kant ultimately sets the stage for a 'historico-critical atti-tude'.[23] As Foucault summarizes the implications, Kant's specific question about the significance of his time and place:

> entails an obvious consequence: that criticism is no longer to be practiced in the search for formal structures with universal value, but rather as a historical investigation into the events that have led us to constitute ourselves and to recognize ourselves as subjects of what we are doing, thinking, saying.[24]

The consequence entailed is, then, a reorientation of the questions of value and intelligibility. A critical approach to these questions asks about the modalities of value and meaning. It shows how valued aspects of life are shaped and represented and inquires into the implications of not only *how* but also *when* a difference with respect to value and meaning is articulated.

In Foucault's time-sensitive, genealogical frame, the 'events' that have produced the modern body, for example, as it is understood in institutionalized interpretations, are arbitrary. Foucault, like Kant, rejects the iconic thing in itself, but rather than displacing the privile-ging of the thing with a 'productive understanding,' responsible for the shape and temporal extension of phenomena, Foucault substitutes a genealogical practice of historical sensibility. His model substitutes 'the haphazard play of domination'[25] for a model in which what exists arises from a progressive history of discovery, as understandings become historically enlarged.

To render Foucault's genealogical perspective relevant to the sport-ing event with which we began, we must turn to a genealogy of the sporting experience. Ray Agnew's slow body is not something that the evolution of wisdom or the growing coherence of cognitive faculties can discover. It is 'slow' because contemporary media, articulated with various other modern institutions, place demands on the dura-tion of representations. Seeing the body, and the interpretations imposed on its motions, as an after-effect of complex structures of power and authority is afforded by a genealogical reading of the history of bodies and spatio-temporalities.

It should be noted in addition that this way of seeing bodies in motion implies a different answer to the question 'what is critique?'[26] from that supplied by Kant. For the Kantian concern with knowledge and legitimation, Foucault substitutes the question of 'power and eventualization'.[27] Paying attention to what he thinks German critical thought has neglected, 'the coercive structure of the signifier',[28] Foucault locates the politics of meaning in imbalances among forces, such that events achieve their intelligibility, at the expense of alternative possible modes of intelligibility. To examine 'eventualization,'[29] is therefore to inquire into the 'mechanisms of coercion'[30] that hover around the contemporary coding of events as experience. This Foucauldian focus encourages us to locate Agnew's performance as a peculiarly contemporary event, shaped by the forces now controlling the sporting experience.

A Brief Genealogy of the Experience of Sports

How, if we heed both the Kantian insights and Foucault's reorientation of the question of critique, can we deepen our appreciation of the power-related temporality of sports? The first step must involve a recognition of the temporally invested legacy of contemporary sports; they have evolved from what were once regarded as 'pastimes'. Although there are various different places at which the narrative could begin in order to locate the significant ruptures that distinguish today's sporting experiences, the departure of sports from ritual,[31] and from its more ludic dimensions, stands out. For the former, the practices of the ancient Greeks provide an exemplary initiating venue, while for the latter, one would do well by investigating the changing balance of forces between play and display that Johan Huizinga observed. Writing in the 1950s, he argued that 'with the increasing systematization and regimentation of sport, something of the pure play-quality is inevitably lost'.[32]

For purposes of capturing the implications of the Agnew event, we should restrict our attention to the relatively recent historical dynamics that Huizinga had in mind. The 'systematization and regimentation' of which he spoke have been grouped and summarized by Norbert Elias as 'sportization,'[33] the historical process through which leisure-time activities, whose attributes had been controlled by (nonprofessional) participants, became subject to various rules and regulations that altered their structures. Elias points out that the current strictures on duration, participation, and venue resulted from all of the forces associated with the commercialization of modern life, with time control and budgeting as the most significant dimensions.

The temporal dimensions of the sports themselves came to be

experienced in the context of the temporal practices of spectators, as time for watching sporting events expanded with changes in the structures of work and leisure. In the earlier part of the twentieth century, sports had their seasons, and spectators associated their trips to various arenas or ballparks with the time of year as well as with the leisure time of the weekend.

The weekend, as a structuring time of experience, however, is a relatively recent invention. Parallel to a history of the sportization of pastimes is the historical production of the sporting spectator, who emerged as the result of two historic victories. The first was the victory of secular authorities over church authorities. Over approximately three centuries, Puritanism and other religious pressures to preserve non-working times for religious observance lost out to the pressures from political leaders, entrepreneurs, and the population at large, to produce a weekend in which leisure and sporting activities and spectatorship became dominant.[34] But the weekend itself could only achieve its temporal specificity as leisure as a result of the second kind of victory, the historic victory of the labour movement to shorten the working week. In sum, 'although play and games have been part of every known society, leisure institutions as a segregated part of life available to the masses required a change in both organizational and cultural values'.[35]

Without dwelling on all of the recent changes associated with the commercialization of sport and the proliferation of the various commodities – both things and persons associated with this stage – the role of media has to be considered as primary. Two analysts of the sport media relationship make this point unequivocally:

> The single most dominant influence on the way sport is experienced in American society is that of the mass media, particularly television.[36]

Recalling Ray Agnew's (slowly) hurtling body, one might say that for a relatively brief moment, *he* had the game under control. But if Lever and Wheeler's attribution about the dominance of television in the production of the sporting experience is correct, the issue of Agnew's control over the game and indeed over his own moving body at other moments becomes more complex.

It is certainly the case that the televisualization of professional sports has displaced other forms of institutional control over non-work time. It was a sign of the times, for example, that the television sports network ESPN's advertisement for its Sunday football game (in the 1980s) showed Oakland Raiders corner back, Lester Haynes, kneeling in a prayerful pose in the Los Angeles Coliseum and accompanied the image with the lines: 'Join our Congregation every Sunday for an inspirational experience.'

The advertisment plays with an interesting anachronism. The 'Congregation' will not physically congregate in church or at the game; it consists rather of remote viewers watching, for the most part, within the confines of their separate dwellings. And of course, the substitution of sports viewing for church attendance (as well as live stadium attendance) has economic correlates. The secularization of formerly religiously affiliated colleges has led, among other things, to more influence over the symbolism of the schools by sports shoe manufacturers than by denominational religious leaders.

The influence of sports clothing manufacturers is of course closely tied to the media–college sports relationship. At the college level, the importance of revenues from television has skewed athletic programmes towards a heavy emphasis on athletic recruitment and has altered the goals of the sports programme. A 'winning season' must include post-season participation. The success of a collegiate sports programme requires the chance of a post-season appearance in a bowl or tournament. A college team must be 'bowl bound' to be telegenic and thereby be able to raise the revenues to have their programme remain competitive,[37] hence their susceptibility to inducements to exclusive sports clothing and shoe contracts. The media-related economic forces behind sports publicity have a more pervasive effect than the older forms of social publicity, religious and political, that participated in shaping the social body.

If we go back to the Kantian model of experience, we can recognize that the ultimate stage, that of publicity, must be understood differently from what is implied in Kant's notion of expanding, shared cognition. The conditions of possibility for publicity involve a complex organization of space, time, economic value, and, ultimately, social meaning that shapes the prior stages of how events are experienced at the level of cognition. The 'matter', which involves hurtling bodies, and the more immediate consequences of the bodies in motion – what counts as a valuable contribution – are significantly affected by the structures of publicity.

Games like football and basketball, for example, have changed their rules to hold the interest of present and remote spectators. And unregulated moves *in* the game by players are affected by the future publicity of the game. For example, one professional basketball player, Scottie Pippen of the Chicago Bulls, when asked, during a post-game interview, why he had not contested an opponent's slam dunk, responded that he did not want his futile defensive gesture to be a post-game highlight.

At that moment, Pippen, a black athlete, functioning in a media-inspired, commercial environment, had seized momentary control over his value by controlling his movements. Similarly, as Giants' tackle, Ray Agnew, also a black athlete, hurtled towards the end zone, his movement and the value that would result were under his control, even though the ultimate value of the experience, which would include its potential for post-game exposure, was not. The compelling value questions are therefore condensed in Ray Agnew's run. How are the power implications of the time–value relationship, immanent in moving black athletic bodies, to be mapped? Moreover, how does an approach to this question help us understand, more generally, 'now-time'?

To approach these questions we must first broaden our gaze to comprehend what precedes as well as what follows from a particular set of movements. More specifically, to analyze the relationship between moving black bodies and value critically, one must extend the game not only into its futurity in media reproductions but also backwards into the dynamics of recruitment. We must analyze the motions produced by the search for the 'black gold'[38] being mined by the sports establishment, from high school to professional levels. Recognizing that the value of the black athlete extends from the games and their media representations to the marketing of game-related products – Michael Jordan is arguably the most globally recognized marketing icon as well as athlete[39] – we must pursue the implications for how various forces that feed off games also participate in inducing movement and producing containment of moving black bodies in the process of collecting them.

Viewed from the perspective of potential professional athletes, the temptation to dream of a professional athletic career, no matter how the odds are stacked against success, is obvious. Given the enormous gap between black social mobility in general and the relative successes of black athletes in sports, the dream of a successful athletic career energizes the sporting play of many young black males in the poor neighbourhoods of US cities. Athletic success is seen as a 'last shot,'[40] as a way out. The affects of those dreams, the mobilization of black bodies that they evince, are portrayed in Steve James, Frederick Marx, and Peter Gilbert's film version (1994), and (Ben Joravsky's subsequent book version, 1995), of *Hoop Dreams*, which follows the high school basketball careers of Arthur Agee and William Gates, two gifted players from a Chicago housing project. The emphasis here is on the film rather than the book version of the story because, in important respects, the cinematic practice – the assemblage of camera shots in *Hoop Dreams* – captures both the motion requirements of the game of basketball and the social-mobility requirements for athletic and monetary success imposed on Arthur and William, the primary personae of the docudrama. To understand how cinematic practice relates to such motions, however, we must preface a consideration of the film with a treatment of the intimate relationship between cinematic time/movement and modernity. This requires another gloss on Kant, that of Gilles Deleuze.

The Deleuzian Gloss

Like Foucault, Deleuze extracts himself from Kant patiently, giving him his due at each juncture. From the point of view of the problematic of temporality, Deleuze recognizes that Kant's contribution, beyond introducing a more productive I/subject, involves the introduction of 'time into thought'.[41] Because for Kant, time is not intrinsic to the world but rather to the productive understanding, Deleuze credits him with supplying a resistance to a progressive model of history. Understanding is a constitutive event not a form of recognition of events that pre-exist the modalities of their conceptual capture.

But Deleuze finds it necessary not only to depart from the Kantian formalism, where time is intrinsic to a universalizing mental faculty, but also from the Kantian emphasis on productive understanding as a mode of *representation*.[42] For Deleuze, one constitutes events politically not merely cognitively. Elaborating on the necessity for leaving Kant's (and empiricism's) emphasis on epistemology behind, Deleuze notes:

> We must then break with the long habit of thought which forces us to consider the problematic as a subjective category of our knowledge or as an empirical moment which would indicate only the imperfection of our method and the unhappy necessity for us not to know ahead of time – a necessity which would disappear once we acquire knowledge.[43]

Events have no determined actuality for Deleuze; they are formed neither in the world nor by structures of subjectivity. Rather, events have a virtual structure that is never captured in any particular determination.[44] Because they offer no natural points of division, they emerge as a result of an imposition. But what is involved in those impositions in which the actual of the event emerges? It is not, as Kant would have it, the imposition of a universalizing intellect. Rather, it is the imposition of what Deleuze and Guattari call 'order-words'.[45] Temporally, at the level of the virtual, the event is continuous. Bodies, for example, grow old. But for a given actualization of the body, there must be specific impositions, expressed in such order-words as: 'you are no longer a child'.[46]

Whereas Kant supplies a universalizing, cognitive status to the ordering faculty or intellect, Deleuze's ordering words should be understood normatively rather than cognitively; they function within a pragmatics and politics of language.[47] To resist a cognitive rendering of the temporality of events-as-actualizations is to resist 'dogmatism'. But Deleuze's resistance to dogmatism is different from Kant's. The dogmatic image of thought, according to Deleuze, is the very idea that 'thought has an affinity with the true'.[48] Thought for Deleuze is not aimed towards a Kantian *sensus communis*; it is aimed, rather, at achieving an uncommon sense. It does not seek 'the truth' but seeks instead to provide vehicles for experiencing the world differently. Accordingly, thought expresses events rather than representing them. Deleuze rejects a commitment to the epistemic authority of common sense because it rests on the presupposition that 'thought is the natural exercise of a faculty,' which has an 'affinity with the true' if we assume '*good will on the part of the thinker* and an *upright nature on the part of thought*.'[49] Deleuze regards this exercise of 'common sense' as recognition rather than thought;[50] it, along with 'good sense' (the contribution of faculties), constitutes the doxa, the unreflected upon acceptance of the world of actualities that exists in everyday, banal discourses.

As a critical enterprise, then, Deleuzian 'thought,' insofar as it resists representation and mere recognition ('common sense'), supplies an uncommon sense. By supplying resistant conceptualizations, it situates us in a place to both map and treat critically the current forces shaping relations of time and value.[51] The question becomes one of the vehicles for the production of thinking-as-uncommon-sense. Among the places towards which Deleuze turns for critical thought vehicles is cinema, which, it in its modern realization, is a mode of articulation that thinks the politics of time and value. It is a critical and disruptive thought enterprise rather than a mechanism of representation, which un-reflectively participates in the production of a *sensus communis*. Kantian reflective judgement relies on the presentational mechanism of mental faculties. Developing his critical philosophy in a pre-cinematic epoch, Kant was unable to share Benjamin's and Deleuze's appreciation of the critical capacity of aesthetic technologies that exceed vision and intellect by reproducing and animating the sensorium. His *sensus communis* is predicated on an integrating judgement, while those who now aim critique at an uncommon sense recognize the way various aesthetic technologies mediate and fragment experience.

Stills and Movement Images

As cinema evolved, the mobile camera ultimately led, as Deleuze notes, to the 'emancipation of the viewpoint,' and, most significantly, to a privileging of time over space. With the use of montage, the assemblage of camera shots: 'The shot would then stop being a spatial category and become a temporal one.'[52] In Deleuze's post-Kantian perspective, then, experiencing events critically in the present is afforded not by the exercise of a faculty of judgement that can integrate the domains controlled by disparate cognitive faculties, but by a cinematic apparatus. Deleuze notes that whereas the meaning of movement in antiquity involved the idea of transition – 'movement refers to intelligible elements, Forms or Ideas which are themselves eternal or immobile'[53] – modernity is an epoch without privileged instants. Movement is understood as a matter of assembling 'any-instant-whatever,'[54] and contemporary cinema enacts modernity's construction of time and movement; it is 'the system which produces movement as a function of any-instant-whatever that is, as a function of equidistant instants, selected so as to create an impression of continuity'.[55] The modern cinema has discovered that the 'time image' constitutes a way of reading events that is more critical than mere perception.[56] As long as the camera merely followed action, the image of time was indirect, presented as a consequence of motion. But the new 'camera consciousness' is no longer defined by the movements it is able to follow. This consciousness, articulated through modern cinema, has become sensitive to a model of time that is more critical than what such a derivative model supplies. Now, 'even when it is mobile, the camera is no longer content to follow the character's movement . . .'[57] It employs the time image to think about the time and value of the present.

The homology that Deleuze posits between cinematic practice and our (critically thoughtful) experience of time-movement of the present

– 'thinking in cinema through cinema'[58] – is best observed when we distance ourselves from the present both historically and cinematically, the former to make the present peculiar and the latter to observe how a time-sensitive, camera consciousness can render any period critically. We need, therefore, to find a more static historical epoch and to analyze a cinematic practice capable of capturing it. This will allow us not only to appreciate the relationship between cinematic practices and the epochs on which they are deployed but also to see the way in which a critical approach to now-time allows us, in Benjamin's terms, to capture an image of the past that 'flashes up at the instant when it can be recognized'.[59]

For this purpose, Stanley Kubrick's film version of Thackerey's *Barry Lyndon* is exemplary. Historically, the action unfolds within a static socio-political culture, the 'estate space' of English aristocracy in the eighteenth century, a time in which the order was almost wholly ascriptive in structure and thought to be a creation of divine will.[60] Various mechanisms were in place to defeat attempts to alter or penetrate that order. And, to complete this contrast, Kubrick is cinematically sensitive to the fixity of the eighteenth-century order. He frequently immobilizes his camera. Moreover, he explicitly acknowledges his understanding of the social–cinematic homology by referring to his cinematographer (in the credits) as a photographer.

Barry Lyndon

William Makepiece Thackerey's *The Memoirs of Barry Lyndon, Esq.* derives much of its critical edge from the narrative voice of its protagonist. The tale that Barry Lyndon recounts does not ring true. As a result, readers are drawn into a critical reflection on the boundary between truth and fiction. The novel makes problematic the interrelationship of text and reader, while, at the same time, satirizing the seriousness with which one would-be social climber takes the value of heritage or pedigree. Written a century after its subject matter, the tale seems more directed towards illuminating the ambiguities of telling tales and distinguishing the telling from history than towards illuminating a particular historical period.[61]

In Kubrick's film version, 'the power of the false'[62] is also enlisted but in the service of a different aim. The protagonist's voice is displaced from narrative control by one of Barry Lyndon's contemporaries, and more importantly, the oral text is superseded by the visual, filmic text. The film viewers are not subjected to an unreliable narrator. Rather, they experience what Deleuze calls a 'crystalline regime,' which he juxtaposes to an organic one.[63] In organic film narration, the objects of filmic description are assumed to be independent. The camera simply follows the action. Organic narration is therefore 'truthful narration,' even if it follows the action of a fictional story.[64] In contrast, in crystalline film narration, the filmic description creates its objects. Chronological time – that which is imposed by following the actors – is displaced by 'non-chronological time,' and movements, which are 'necessarily "abnormal"' are 'essentially false'.[65] The experience created, in short, is a function of the assemblage of camera shots. Instead of composing movement images to treat the tensions explicitly acknowledged by the actors, the camera creates time images that respond to the critical thinking of the orchestrated cinematic apparatus rather than the modes of consciousness of the film's characters.

More specifically, constructed in the modern period, Kubrick's camera work renders the eighteenth century from the point of view of the present. The comparison implies that while modernity is cinematic, the eighteenth century was more painterly or photographic, that modernity is to the eighteenth century as the film genre is to those of painting and photography.

Frank Cossa has provided supporting insights to such a comparison, discerning the pervasiveness of art-historical referents of eighteenth-century life in the film:

> Lady Lyndon (Marisa Berenson) . . . is dressed and coiffed like the ladies in Gainsborough portraits . . . the famous candlelit interiors in the film resemble those of Joseph Wright of Derby . . . The crystal grey tonalities in many of the daylight interiors call to mind the genre paintings of both Chardin and Greuze [and] when a groom trots out a horse that Barry (Ryan O'Neal) will buy for his son, groom and horse strike a pose reminiscent of George Stubbs' portraits of famous racehorses of the day.[66]

Insofar as Kubrick is establishing a homology between technologies of representation and modalities of sociability, it is inapposite to complain, as one reviewer did, that *Barry Lyndon* is 'a triumph of technique over any human content'.[67] It is the case, rather, that Kubrick's filmic technique constitutes the content. The deceptions of Kubrick's Barry Lyndon are less significant than the aristocratic practices of time and space that are revealed as Redmond Barry, an Irishman with a questionable pedigree, attempts to insinuate himself in English estate society.

That society is presented, through the camera work, in terms of its forms and slow, ritualistic pacing. Even the battle scenes, which on the basis of body count are very bloody, come across as rigidly organized death rituals. What one observes is a society that preserves its static structures of privilege by absorbing and defeating movement. And Kubrick's camera articulates this stasis as the film explores, with framing and zoom shots, massed armies, large estates, ornate interiors, and wall paintings, capturing them in a series of *tableaux vivants*. Through the ensemble of shots, the animate is continually overmastered by the inanimate.

The estates in *Barry Lyndon* are shot frontally; they are made to appear as they do in eighteenth-century engravings. Pedigree is represented through various still portraits. And in the midst of the stasis and restraint of the eighteenth-century English society, an ambitious Barry Lyndon tries to move in and upwards, aiming to achieve an aristocratic status. His failure 'to acquire aristocratic restraint'[68] ultimately defeats him. Unable to manage the slow, ritualistic decorum of the society to which he seeks admission, Barry Lyndon is finally stopped by a bullet in a duel. He could have shot his adversary, Lord Bullington, but is shot himself and ultimately is immobilized, losing a leg.

All of the structural elements leading to Barry Lyndon's failure are captured cinematographically. Most of the shots are taken with a static camera. While the framed shots and zooms are wholly appropriate for representing the stasis of the social order, even the use of montage reflects a lack of motion in that order. Rather than conveying action in the form of movement through time, montage in Barry Lyndon is referential.[69] Duelling scenes occur at the beginning and end of the film, the latter recalling the former. Highly stylized scenes of kissing and embracing at many points throughout the film, more than a dozen of which involve Barry Lyndon, have the effect of demonstrating the perseverance of ceremonial forms rather than the social progress of the protagonist. Although Barry Lyndon does manage to rise up the social ladder for a while, his inability to adopt the correct forms leads to his fall. His failure to fit correctly within the frames of his century is represented figuratively in a scene in which the film-as-still-pictures focuses on Barry Lyndon's attempt to acquire pictures (at exorbitant prices according to the voice-over narration). As Barry Lyndon ambles slowly through a room with many elegantly framed paintings, the room, containing an ensemble of stills, seems to reflect the spatio-temporal zone, English estate society, in which he is striving for a peerage.

It is made clear, moreover, that in the eighteenth-century world, money alone will not produce the desired status movement. Movement and time are ordered by a moral economy that helps preserve the connection between birth and fortune. Nothing testifies better to this static arrangement than a scene in which the aristocratic Bullington family, into which Barry Lyndon has married, is going over its accounts. Seated with them is their friend and confidante, the Reverent Runt, who is beside Lady Lyndon along with Lord Bullington, Barry's stepson, the rightful heir, while she signs her bills in a *tableau vivant*, captured by a still camera.

Kubrick's immobilized camera does not, however, immobilize thought. It participates in providing a politics of time. For example, the frequent resort to a depth-of-field shot – shots in which current action is unfolding in front of enduring residences, ancestral paintings, and managed estate grounds – has the effect of showing those things that have time on their side as the more effectual background against which the mere striving-motion of a Barry Lyndon is futile.[70] More generally, as Deleuze points out, even when a shot remains immobile, it can fracture the illusion that space is wholly separate from time, a mere container of actions and the illusion that time simply chronologically records the process of evoking and resolving the tensions, which are explicitly acknowledged by those who participate in them.[71] The camera has access to what the characters do not: a thinking of time not in terms of its derivation from the chronology of action but in terms of the juxtapositions necessary to render problematic the forces at work and the intersections of those forces as they emanate from different layers in time.[72]

Hoop Dreams

In contrast with the filmic technique in *Barry Lyndon, Hoop Dreams* contains a majority of tracking shots as the viewer watches the attempts of Arthur Agee and William Gates to use their basketball skills to escape from their impoverished housing project and realize their shared dream of playing professional basketball. Speed rather than restraint and decorum are demanded of them, but to appreciate the prescribed movement they must achieve to realize their goals, we have to be attentive not only to their particular biographies, on which the film focuses, but also to the movement demands of modernity in general. The opening shots, while the credits are run, show the rapid motion demands of the present. Chicago's moving traffic – trains, cars, trucks, and buses – crisscross our view of the city.

The movement of vehicles with which the film begins is the beginning of a camera consciousness that operates throughout *Hoop Dreams* to provide a gloss on the politics of the collection of black bodies for professional sports. Although the camera consciousness deployed in *Hoop Dreams* is very different from its realization in *Barry Lyndon*, it nevertheless supplies a politicized reading of contemporary time–value relationships. What must be understood to situate this reading is that power manifests itself differently in the twentieth century from the way it did in the eighteenth. Since the French Revolution, the structures of domination have changed their modalities.

If we note that the French Revolution was the most dramatic assault on the aristocracy's management of the stasis governing the European society of the eighteenth century, Paul Virilio's gloss on the events beginning in 1789 become especially appropriate. He asserts that the revolution, far from ending subjection in general, was rather a revolution against the '*constraint to immobility*'.[73] Thereafter, with the birth of the modern state, the '*freedom of movement*'[74] of the early days of the revolution had been turned, by the exercise of state power, to an '*obligation to mobility*,'[75] as the state involved itself in, among other things, the recruitment and mobilization of a citizen army.

Subsequently, of course, commercial forces have been at least as involved in the mobilization of bodies as the state and certainly more so in the case of the movement that nourishes sporting franchises. What must be added to this picture of mobilization are the moving frames within which the movements constituting the present life-world are witnessed. The motion of the sporting bodies – from recruitment to performance and subsequent publicity – must be understood in the context of the way that motion is apprehended through modern media. Oliver Wendell Holmes, who observed the early, photographic stages of the cinematic society, conveniently glossed modernity-as-experience in an idiom that summons Kant's categories but revises the relationship between the form-imposing faculties and the matter they apprehend:

> Form is henceforth divorced from matter. In fact matter as a visible object is of no great use any longer, except as the mold on which form is shaped. Give us a few negatives of a thing worth seeing, taken from different points of view, and that is all we want of it.[76]

As Holmes understood, 'modernity' is a new kind of structure of experience. The modern city, as a venue of hyper-stimuli, places pressures on the Kantian reliance on faculties that tend towards a universal common sense. Jonathan Crary seconds this observation, noting, 'since Kant . . . part of the epistemological dilemma of modernity has been about the human capacity for synthesis amid fragmentation and atomization of a cognitive field'.[77] But here, Crary renders the issue too much in Kantian terms. Rather than assuming that experience is formed and contained by a cognitive capacity, we must recognize (as Crary does in other parts of his analysis) the extent to which 'experience' is owed to technologies of representation and reproduction.

Whatever the relative contributions of human cognition and technology-induced forms in the constitution of experience, there is a strong homology between the structure of filmic representation and modern life. No one has recognized this homology more profoundly than Walter Benjamin: 'The film,' he stated, 'corresponds to profound changes in the apperceptive apparatus – changes that are experienced on an individual scale by the man in the street in big-city traffic, on a historical scale by every present-day citizen.'[78]

With Benjamin's insight in mind we can better appreciate the contemporary experience of sports, both from the point of view of those seeking entry into the rewards of playing for a high level of remuneration and those who watch games and enact their connection with them by buying sports shoes and clothing. Benjamin recognized that as exhibition value displaces ritual value in a variety of contexts,[79] market value intervenes and wrests control over the meaning of a performance, whether it is enacted in a feature film or a sporting contest.[80]

We are now in a position to locate the value deriving from what Virilio called the modernity's 'obligation to mobility' as it applies to Arthur Agee and William Gates in *Hoop Dreams*. At a minimum, the contemporary demands for mobility and the correlative demands on 'apperceptive apparatuses' are so familiar to us, it is easy to miss the extent to which *Hoop Dreams* captures the modern experience of sports more with its camera work than with its storyline.

At a thematic level, the story has a familiar theme. Arthur and William see their basketball skills as their opportunity to be part of the American dream; they hope to make it all the way into the status of professionals, as players in the National Basketball Association (NBA). And because a black recruiter, with contacts in a white private high school with big-time basketball aspirations, has a similar view of their skills, they end up enrolling in the school. The film is, among other things, an ethnography of both the venues in which they reside and those they must traverse in their quest. It effectively maps the spaces and living relationships in their impoverished black neighbourhood, in white suburbia, and in the competitive basketball venues of high schools and colleges, which all participate in the structural recruitment of black athletes.[81]

Arthur and William must move rapidly, not only on the basketball court but also in the process of moving through discordant social spaces. The normalizing pressures that exist within their black neighbourhoods, for example, are quite different from those that structure performances in the white high school they attend after being recruited for their basketball skills.[82] This structural story, told by the camera, can be missed if one simply follows the drama associated with Arthur and William's attempts to achieve the status of professional basketball players.

For example, Jillian Sandell's highly politicized reading of the film fails to appreciate how it works, because the reading is wholly thematic. The problem of neglecting filmic form surfaces early in an otherwise effective gloss of the story:

> Spotted by talent scouts when they are 14, Arthur and William are offered scholarships to attend St. Joseph's College – a predominantly white, Catholic private school in suburban Westchester and the alma mater of Detroit Pistons' star, Isaiah Thomas . . . The central conceit of *Hoop Dreams* is whether Arthur and/or William will become 'the next Isaiah Thomas.' Both boys must get up at 5:30 A.M. to make the three-hour round trip to St. Joseph's . . . and this is a testament to the work ethic and sense of sacrifice that the film valorizes.[83]

Sandell may be correct that the pleasure the film delivers to white audiences derives from their witnessing of a story about two young African-Americans seeking a piece of the American dream, but in addition to the 'organic narrative', which follows the striving of Arthur and William, is the 'crystalline narrative' assembled by the various camera shots. Sandell neglects this narrative because her focus is on representational space rather than cinematically thought time. She notes that the black urban experience provides a *space* for film-makers to treat issues of cultural life in the ghetto,[84] for example, but fails to treat the way the mobile camera renders movements through space and provides a critical, non-chronological view of time. By cutting from the time of basketball games to the temporalities of family life, to the temporalities of the educational process, and emphasizing both conjunctures and disjunctions, the camera consciousness in *Hoop Dreams* 'invents,' in Deleuze's terms, a 'transverse continuity of communication' between different temporal layers.[85] Rather than merely representing a sequence of events, the film seizes Arthur's and William's experiences and connects them to a politics and ethics of modernity. While it shows spaces and bodies, it thinks time and value.

The film can therefore be seen as an effective event when it is thought of as rendering aspects of mobility rather than merely exploring spaces. If we follow the camera, particularly its tracking shots and its cuts and juxtapositions (montage), we learn that success is denied to Arthur and William because they cannot move fast enough. On the one hand, the American dream, reflected through the promotion of a narrative about playing your way into the NBA, produces an incitement to mobility, but on the other hand, their need to move rapidly through discordant social spaces obviates the realization of that dream. There is the travel time required to get to St. Joseph's; there is the difficulty of learning the kind of articulations demanded in the classroom and on the court in dealing with white culture; and there are the academic demands on young men without cultural capital. Their progress is impeded by these barriers to rapid motion.

Arthur is also frustrated by his biological clock; he fails to grow rapidly enough to impress St. Joseph's coach, and ultimately his scholarship is cut to the point where he must drop out of the school. Afterwards, he manages to move rapidly enough through academic space in the city school and on the court to push his inner city, predominantly black high school to the finals of the state championships, but all his rapid motion on the court is ultimately inadequate because he is unable to achieve the social mobility necessary to place him in a more visible trajectory through the sporting establishment.

The fate of William Gates, who appears more promising to the white basketball establishment at St. Joseph's, bears a striking resemblance to the fate of Barry Lyndon. William manages to stay at St. Joseph's and is recruited by Marquette University, a traditional major college basketball power, but he is ultimately defeated because a knee injury slows him down. Barry Lyndon's loss of his leg is symbolic. *His* immobility reflects the immobility of the aristocratic structure. After his moving fails to penetrate the stasis of eighteenth-century English society, his final immobility is ironic and allegorical.

William's loss of mobility handicaps him in the race to achieve an NBA level of playing ability. But he shows just enough promise to acquire help from the white establishment in moving over the academic hurdles; he manages to qualify for a basketball scholarship. William can move well enough to constitute 'black gold' – to be a potential resource in the marketing of a basketball programme – but the potential is never realized. His college athletic career is not impressive enough to project him into the professional ranks.

Most significantly, the narrative conveyed by the cinematic practice does not at all valorize the 'American dream'. The framing shots in *Barry Lyndon* are to the structure of power and authority in the eighteenth century as the tracking shots in *Hoop Dreams* are to that structure in the late twentieth. Barry Lyndon, the marginal Irishman without pedigree, is defeated by stasis, while the marginal black would-be basketball stars, Arthur and William, without cultural and economic capital, are defeated by their inability to get up to speed in modernity's implacable 'obligation to mobility'. Finally, in terms of the comparison of the filmic thoughts about the respective centuries, while the montage effects in *Barry Lyndon* are referential, serving to underscore the perseverance of static structures, the montage effects in *Hoop Dreams* provide a lesson in the political economy modern sports. The rapid cut from Arthur watching professional basketball on television to Arthur on the playground, seeking to enact the movement himself, shows, for example, the way the exhibition of sports mobilizes a would-be star. And equally significant is the cut from scenes of playing basketball and watching basketball to one of the most telling scenes in the film: the camera suddenly captures a group of young black males walking down the street in new, expensive basketball shoes.

The mobility of exemplary stars on the court is ultimately realized in the movement of sporting goods. Some of the 'black gold' turns out to be located in a different mine; it is the one holding consumers, the young black males who enact their dreams symbolically by buying clothes and shoes. Indeed, the political economy of 'black gold' is shown through montage pervasively. In stark comparison with the moral economy of eighteenth-century life, where a priest helps to preside over the account books, is the use of a machine calculator on the desk of St. Joseph's fiscal officer. When Arthur and his parents revisit the school to get his transcript released, the fiscal officer recalculates their payment schedule and suggests that they must make some payments on the new schedule to show 'good faith', where economic 'good faith' is strictly a budgeting concept, tied to a rate of repayment.

Ultimately, by resisting a simple thematic reading of *Hoop Dreams* and lodging it instead in a comparison of the temporal practices of different ages, it becomes an important event. It reminds us not only of the extent to which modern life can be critically rendered cinematically but also the extent to which the contemporary experience of sports relies in part on the exploitation of moving black bodies.[86] In Benjamin's spirit, we are able to see the present in the past, not on the basis of a simple continuum but 'through a leap in the open air of history'.[87] This leap, along with a genealogical imagination and the philosophy of concepts guiding the comparison, landed us in the midst of a politics of now-time. As Deleuze and Guattari have put it, 'what philosophy achieves when it extracts events from the clashes of bodies and things is the "counter-effectuation" of the event'.[88] Ray Agnew's run therefore changes from a mere sports news item to a politicized event within a conceptual terrain that allows us to ask what is different about today. We are able to note that the contemporary experience of sports is, among other things, reflected in moving black bodies – on playing fields, in the social order, and in the streets (clothed and shod in sports-logo apparel). Those motions represent an important aspect of contemporary power: an imposition of an 'obligation to mobility'.

Notes

1. Mike Freeman, 'Pontiac, Michigan, Oct. 27: Giants Crush Inept Lions in the Dome,' *New York Times*, 1996 October 28, p. B7.
2. Walter Benjamin, 'Theses on the Philosophy of History', in *Illuminations* trans. Harry Zohn (New York: Harcourt, Brace and World, 1968), p. 261.
3. Ibid., p. 255.
4. Walter Benjamin, 'On the Program of the Coming Philosophy', in Gary Smith (ed.), *Benjamin: Philosophy, History, Aesthetics* (Chicago: University of Chicago Press, 1989), p. 1.
5. Immanuel Kant, *Critique of Pure Reason*, trans. J. M. D. Meiklejohn (London: George Bell and Sons, 1876), p. 99.
6. Kant uses a geo-political/governmental metaphor to describe the separation of powers and territorial jurisdictions between different cognitive faculties in the introduction to his third critique. Each exercises, he says, 'legislative authority' over the concepts

residing in their respective territories: *Critique of Judgement*, trans. James Creed Meredith (Oxford: Clarendon Press, 1952), p. 12.

7. Ibid., p. 151.

8. What the notion of understanding, which Kant elaborated in his *First Critique*, does, as one sensitive reader of narratives has suggested, is replace 'the untenable iconic "thing-in-itself" ' with a narrative of phenomena, which is, in effect, 'a model that is not subject to closure'. The quotations are from Geza von Molar, 'Iconic Closure and Narrative Opening in Lessing, Kant, Goethe, and Novalis', *Historical Reflections*, 18 (1992), p 98.

9. This expression is used in Immanuel Kant, *Anthropology from a Pragmatic Point of View*, trans. Victor Lyle Dowdell (Carbondale: Southern Illinois University Press, 1978), p. 40.

10. This sequence is offered in Kant's *Critique of Judgement*, but it is most clearly presented in his *Anthropology from a Pragmatic Point of View*, from which the quotations in this section are taken: p. 29. It should be noted, however, that although Kant's narrative of experience begins with sensation, he also noted instances in which a sensation derives from a concept: see his *Critique of Practical Reason*, p. 95 (trans. Lewis White Beck).

11. Ibid.

12. Kant, *Critique of Judgement*, p. 56.

13. Ibid., p. 154.

14. Ibid., p. 155.

15. Ibid., p. 151.

16. Ibid., p. 152.

17. Ibid., p. 153.

18. Immanuel Kant, 'Perpetual Peace', trans. H. B. Nisbet in Hans Reiss (ed.), *Kant: Political Writings* (New York: Cambridge University Press, 1991), pp. 107–8.

19. Immanuel Kant, 'The Contest of Faculties', in Reiss (ed.), *Kant: Political Writings*, p. 181.

20. Friedrich Nietzsche, *Beyond Good and Evil*, trans. R. J. Hollingdale (Baltimore: Penguin, 1974), no. 211, p. 123.

21. As David Lloyd points out, although much of Kant's *Critique of Judgement* was aimed at providing a universalistic and timeless basis for understanding, his approach to judgement was also very much influenced by his reflection on his particular historical location, 'the disintegrating post-feudal condition of late eighteenth-century Germany.' And, as Lloyd notes,

his turn to examples often undercut the universal model of experience he sought to provide: 'Kant's Examples', *Representations*, 28 (1989), p. 34.

22. Michel Foucault, 'What is Enlightenment?', in Paul Rabinow and William M. Sullivan (eds.), *Interpretive Social Science: A Second Look* (Berkeley: University of California Press, 1987), p. 159.
23. Ibid., p. 171.
24. Ibid., p. 170.
25. Michel Foucault, 'Nietzsche, Genealogy, History', trans. Donald F. Bouchard and Sherry Simon, in Rabinow (ed.), *The Foucault Reader* (New York: Pantheon, 1984), p. 83.
26. See Michel Foucault, 'What is Critique?', trans. Lysa Hochroth, in Sylvere Lotringer and Lysa Hochroth eds., *The Politics of Truth*, ed. (New York: Semiotext(e), 1997), pp. 23–82.
27. Ibid., p. 59.
28. Ibid., p. 42.
29. Ibid., p. 49.
30. Ibid., p. 50.
31. This dynamic has been described in Allen Guttman, *From Ritual to Record* (New York: Columbia University Press, 1978).
32. Johan Huizinga, *Homo Ludens* (Boston: Beacon Press, 1955), p. 197.
33. Norbert Elias, 'Sport as a Sociological Problem', in Norbert Elias and Eric Dunning (eds),*Quest for Excitement* (Oxford: Basil Blackwell, 1986), pp. 126–49
34. This process is chronicled in Denis Brailsford, *Sport, Time, and Society* (New York: Routledge, 1991), p. 52.
35. Janet Lever and Stanton Wheeler, 'Mass Media and the Experience of Sport', *Communication Research*, 20 (1993), p. 126.
36. Ibid., p. 125.
37. Guttman, *From Ritual to Record*, p. 139.
38. The expression belongs to John Hoberman, *Darwin's Athletes* (New York: Houghton Mifflin, 1996).
39. For analysis of the Jordan phenomenon, see the monograph issue of the *Sociology of Sports Journal*, 13:1 (1996).
40. See Darcey Frey's ethnography of the aspirations of black athletes and their families in the Coney Island section of Brooklyn: 'The Last Shot', *Harpers*, no. 286 (1993), pp. 37–60, and *The Last Shot* (New York: Simon and Schuster, 1994).
41. Gilles Deleuze, *Difference and Repetition*, Paul Patton trans. (New York: Columbia University Press, 1994), p. 87.

42. Although the Kantian epistemological frame is representational in the first and second critiques, even though the model departs from the sensationalism of empiricist approaches, in his *Critique of Judgement*, the process that Kant calls a 'representational activity' (p. 151) involves not merely an apprehension of objects. The emphasis is on the co-ordination among different domains of apprehension and has elements of reflection and communication as well. Moreover, in the case of the sublime, 'representation' has no object and no representational consummation: 'that which is apprehended' is, Kant asserts, 'inherently contra-final' (p. 92). If we heed Kant's treatment of sublimity, it becomes difficult, then, to quarantine his approach to understanding within a traditional notion of representation.

43. Gilles Deleuze, *The Logic of Sense*, trans. Mark Lester (New York: Columbia University Press, 1990), p. 54.

44. See Gilles Deleuze and Félix Guattari, *What is Philosophy?*, trans. Hugh Tomlinson and Graham Burchell (New York: Columbia University Press, 1994) for the treatment of events. This part of my reading of Deleuze benefits from Paul Patton's glosses on 'events'. See his essays: 'Concept and Event', *Man and World*, 29 (1996), pp. 315–26 and 'The World Seen From Within: Deleuze and the Philosophy of Events', *Theory and Event*, 1: 1 (1997), http://muse.jhu.edu/journals/tae/.

45. Gilles Deleuze, and Félix Guattari, *A Thousand Plateaus*, trans. Brian Massumi (Minneapolis: University of Minnesota Press, 1987), p. 81.

46. Ibid.

47. Ibid., p. 82.

48. Deleuze, *Difference and Repetition*, p. 131.

49. Ibid.

50. Ibid., p. 133.

51. For a discussion of Deleuze and the politics of time, see Todd May, 'Gilles Deleuze and the Politics of Time', *Man and World*, 29 (1996), pp. 293–304.

52. Gilles Deleuze, *Cinema 1*, trans. Hugh Tomlinson and Barbara Habberjam (London: Athlone, 1986), p. 3.

53. Ibid., p. 4.

54. Ibid.

55. Ibid., p. 5.

56. Gilles Deleuze, *Cinema 2*, trans. Hugh Tomlinson and Robert Galeta (London: Athlone, 1989), p. 24.

57. Ibid., p. 23.

58. Ibid., p. 165.

59. Benjamin, 'Theses on the Philosophy of History', p. 255.

60. For a treatment of this aspect of estate space, see Donald Lowe, *History of Bourgeois Perception* (Chicago: University of Chicago Press, 1982).

61. These observations on Thackerey's novel have been aided by Robert P. Fletcher's analysis: ' "Proving a thing even while you contradict it": Fictions, Beliefs, and Legitimation in *The Memoirs of Barry Lyndon, Esq.*', *Studies in the Novel*, 27 (1995), pp. 493–514.

62. This part of the discussion is edified by Deleuze's observations in *Cinema 2* under the rubric of 'The Powers of the false', pp. 126–55. A good discussion of the Nietzschean influence on this aspect of Deleuze's approach to cinema can be found in D. W. Rodowick, *Gilles Deleuze's Time Machine* (Durham, NC.: Duke University Press, 1997).

63. Deleuze, *Cinema 2*, p. 126.

64. Ibid., p. 127.

65. Ibid., p. 129.

66. Frank Cossa, 'Images of Perfection: Life Imitates Art in Kubrick's *Barry Lyndon*', *Eighteenth Century Life*, 19 (1995), p. 79.

67. Quoted in Benjamin Ross, 'Eternal Yearning', *Sight and Sound* (October 1995), p. 42.

68. Cossa, 'Images of Perfection: Life Imitates Art in Kubrick's *Barry Lyndon*', p. 81.

69. I owe the ascription of a 'referential montage' technique and the insights into its use in various parts of Kubrick's *Barry Lyndon* to John Engell's analysis: '*Barry Lyndon*, a Picture of Irony', *Eighteenth Century Life*, 19 (1995), pp. 83–8.

70. See Deleuze's discussion in *Cinema 2* of the critical thought implications of the depth-of-field shot, pp. 108–25.

71. Ibid., p. 128.

72. Deleuze notes how the camera, 'instead of composing movement images . . . decomposes the relations in a direct time-image in such a way that all possible movements emerge from it'. Ibid., p. 130.

73. Paul Virilio, *Speed and Politics*, trans. Mark Polizzotti (New York: Semiotext(e), 1986), p. 29.

74. Ibid., p. 30.

75. Ibid.

76. Oliver Wendell Holmes, 'The Stereoscope and the Stereograph', in Alan Trachtenberg (ed.), *Essays on Photography* (New Haven: Leete's Island Books, 1980), p. 80.

77. Jonathan Crary, 'Unbinding Vision: Manet and the Attentive Observer in the Late Nineteenth Century', in Leo Charney and Vanessa R. Schwartz (eds), *Cinema and the Invention of Modern Life* (Berkeley: University of California Press, 1995), p. 47.

78. Walter Benjamin, 'The Work of Art in the Age of Mechanical Reproduction', in *Illuminations*, p. 250.

79. Ibid., p. 223.

80. Ibid., p. 231.

81. bell hooks also views the film as an ethnography. Although she derides the way the film valorizes 'the American dream', she also recognizes that it has moments that 'subversively document the way in which these young, black male bodies are callously objectified and dehumanized by the white-male dominated world of sports administration in America': 'Dreams Conquest', *Sight and Sound*, 5 (1995), p. 22.

82. This characterization of movement through discordant social spaces is inspired by an analysis of the disjunctive performance demands on 'stone butches', in their movement through the social network, by Judith Halberstam, 'Lesbian Masculinities: or Even Stone Butches Get the Blues', *Women and Performance*, 8 (1996), pp. 61–73.

83. Jillian Sandell, 'Out of the Ghetto and into the Marketplace: *Hoop Dreams* and the Commodification of Marginality', *Socialist Review*, 25:2 (1995), p. 59.

84. Ibid., p. 57.

85. Deleuze, *Cinema 2*, p. 123.

86. Ray Agnew may be repeating his performance for the Giants but for a lower salary than his seniority would have commanded. In June 1997 he was 'released'. Because of the 'salary cap' within which the National Football League works, he became an expensive black body. He was subsequently rehired at a salary level predicated on no seniority.

87. Benjamin, 'Theses on the Philosophy of History', p. 261.

88. Deleuze and Guattari, *What is Philosophy?*, p. 34.

Hoop Dreams (BFI Stills, Posters and Designs)

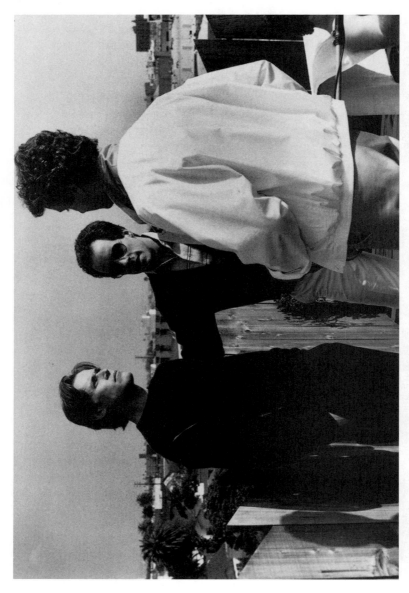

To Live and Die in LA (BFI Stills, Posters and Designs)

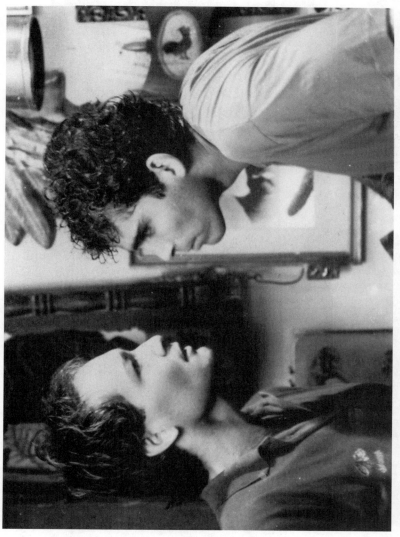

Strawberry and Chocolate (Frasa Y Chocolate) (BFI Stills, Posters and Designs)

The Adventures of Priscilla Queen of the Desert (BFI Stills, Posters and Designs)

2

Narrating the Nation, Unwelcoming the Stranger

Introduction:
Twentieth-century American Jeremiads

In his *Perpetual Peace*, Immanuel Kant predicated his model of global hospitality on the necessity for nations to tolerate difference within themselves as well as in their relationships with other nations.[1] At the same time, however, he recognized the tendency for hostility towards difference to obtain. The goal of a global system, 'united by cosmopolitan bonds' could not be expected if one relied on 'the free consent of individuals'.[2] As a result, Kant's hoped-for cosmopolitan hospitality required laws accompanied by a coercive power that would prevent citizens of a nation from harming people crossing their borders. In Chapter 3, I interrogate the Kantian conception of hospitality and rework it in the light of various post-Kantian perspectives, while, at the same time, directing an encounter between Kantian hospitality and an inhospitable, security-mindedness. In this chapter, I interrogate attachments to the idea of a cultural nation within the state and its connection with the abjection of immigrants. While the nation-state is in focus, I will allow hospitality to stand simply for a welcoming of strangers in the land.

My scene of writing opens on a radically inhospitable climate in the USA. Despite Kant's faith in legal coercion and his optimistic reading of the 'signs of the times', which would promise a future of global peace and hospitality, many contemporary political and legal initiatives militate against recent arrivals from foreign lands. In contrast with Kant's hope for a legally enforced acceptance of cultural difference, in the USA in 1994, as part of an intensifying war on immigrants, 'House Republicans pledged, in their Contract with America, to cut off virtually all welfare benefits for legal immigrants who are under 75 years old.'[3] And subsequently, the war was extended to foreign tongues; a House committee approved a bill 'making English the official language of the United States'.[4]

Throughout 'American' history, 'strangers in the land'[5] have been subjected to a variety of anxiety-driven forms of hostile scrutiny and policy initiative. During the period of the passage of the Alien and Sedition Acts, at the end of the eighteenth century, for example, the Federalists whipped up an anti-immigrant hysteria, arguing that 'the root of all evil in the United States was the large foreign-born population,' that would 'contaminate the purity and simplicity of the American character'.[6]

The contemporary political climate, which encourages attacks from various segments of the social and political order (right-wing journalists, nativist groups, regional labour organizations, state governors, national leaders and legislative bodies), is part of a venerable American tradition. If there is a consistent impetus to the various episodes of an anti-immigrant initiative in the history of USA politics, it is to be found in the cultural anxieties that the actions and articulations reflect. Alien-others, who in various periods, have been 'Indians', French-speakers, Catholics, Irish, southern Europeans, eastern Europeans, Asians, and Third World immigrants, and, in the 1990s, 'illegal aliens' crossing the US border with Mexico, have been constructed as threats to valued models of personhood and to images of a unified national society and culture.

These images have historical and ontological depth; they are continuously recycled in the narratives that constitute the USA as the nation part of the 'nation-state'. While states are understood as territorial entities, the primary understanding of the modern nation portion of the hyphenated term is that it embodies a coherent culture, united on the basis of shared descent or at least that it incorporates a 'people' with a historically stable coherence. As a result, although immigrants are seen from a rationalistic standpoint as competitors for jobs, more significantly, they constitute a disturbance to the mythic stories with which states are alleged to contain single nations. They are perceived as threats by those who seek identity exclusivity in their nation-state attachment. Immigrants therefore both challenge national stories and attract warranting attention from an authority (the state) that many want to appropriate for purposes of individual and collective identity affirmation.

The contemporary scene has special resonance when juxtaposed to similar ones in the past. Historical distance, when paired with the present, introduces a time image that provides an opportunity to situate critically the predicates and modalities of expression of the current anxieties. If, for example, we leap back to the early decades of the twentieth century, we find a much-read academic and trade book treatment of the threat of immigration to America's national culture. The then eminent sociologist E. A. Ross equated policies that allowed a rapid influx of immigrants into the United States with 'race suicide'.[7]

Certainly the 'race' expression is jarring in the context of what is now acceptable academic and journalistic discourse about the effects of immigration. Today's 'meta-racists'[8] explicitly deny that they are focusing on race and refer instead to 'national suicide',[9] or cultural suicide.[10] But another aspect of Ross's polemic is worthy of attention. It conveys a remarkable reliance on evidence of the senses. Ross seems to have felt that he required no epistemic authority for his views beyond what he (as a trained sociologist) could *see*:

> To the practised eye, the physiognomy of certain groups unmistakably proclaims inferiority of type. I have seen gatherings of the foreign-born in which narrow and sloping foreheads were the rule . . . There were so many sugar-loaf heads, moon-faces, lantern jaws, and goose-bill noses that one might imagine a malicious jinn had amused himself by casting human beings in a set of skew-molds discarded by the Creator.[11]

And Ross performed his eye-witness ethnography in a variety of venues:

> That the new immigrants are inferior in looks to the old immigrants may be seen by comparing, in a labor day parade, the faces of the cigar-makers and the garment workers with those of the teamsters, piano-movers and steam-fitters.[12]

Doubtless, Ross saw himself and his 'practised eye' as self-made. But however he might have wanted to imagine himself as a 'self-made man', reliant only on systematic methods rather than a traditional form of bigotry, Ross's 'practised eye' reflects a historically produced assemblage of perspectives: epistemological models of the subject, geographic imaginaries, ethnographic 'knowledge', spatial and economic histories, and national narratives, among others. A summoning here of the various ideational contexts within which Ross's gaze was trained will help-frame a critical approach to the threat of the alien-other, an approach that, in the Kantian sense, seeks the conditions of possibility for a hospitable attitude towards difference.

Ross's confidence in his gaze owes much to a historical transition that took place in the nineteenth century. Whereas subjective vision was suspect during the prior two centuries, the situation of the observer during the nineteenth 'depended on the priority of models of subjective vision'.[13] And, most significantly, the observer that had been created in that century was throughly implicated in the variety of social and economic forces. It was an 'ambulatory observer' taking in the sights within the 'new urban spaces'.[14] The content of Ross's gaze cannot be understood as simply mirroring what he observed; it was 'an *effect* of a heterogeneous network of discursive, social, technological, and institutional relations'.[15] More specifically, in addition to a prevailing discourse on race and nationality, a history of American industrial growth and the migratory effects it encouraged was implicated in Ross's reports about what he saw. Various industries had drawn immigrants from different parts of the globe, and different groups displayed different vulnerabilities to exploitation and confronted differing levels of exclusion.

Ross's complaints about un-assimilable races functioned within a domain of 'knowledge' and a spatially predicated story. What he *saw* reflected a convergence in the twentieth century of racial science and racial nationalism.[16] He wholly accepted and recycled an already scientifically questioned typology of racial characteristics, and his model of global space privileged a nation-state, geo-political cartography.

Moving back to the present, we observe today's immigration alarmists arguing on cultural rather than race/biological grounds. They invoke an amalgam of undigested sociologisms, anthropologisms and political theories (from Tocqueville onward) to question the ability of American society to assimilate culturally the current influx of people to an American 'cultural core', which they posit as a predicate of both the American democratic ethos and the functioning of the American economy.[17] Moreover, in keeping with their shift from the science of race to the social science of cultural assimilation, they evince none of Ross's confidence in subjective perception. What was for Ross a very specific, bodily threat has become a demographic one. The strange bodies have become abstracted and assembled. The threat is to America's demographic entity, a 'population', not to an exemplary and sightly citizen body.[18]

By the time the contemporary Ross's (the 1990s immigration alarmists) arrived on the scene, an altered epistemic regime was in place. The once visible ethnoscape had been replaced by conceptual and statistical abstractions. Certainly, aspects of the discourse of racial science remain. Allen Brimelow, for example, often refers to 'stock', but rather than emphasizing an influx of different racial types, he employs locational and anthropological tropes, referring for example to 'four "cultural hearths" . . . delineated by linguistic geographers',[19] from which American cultural diversity had been constructed by mid-twentieth century. This, manageable level of diversity is a comfortable 'balance' for Brimelow. He sees the current influx threatening to destabilize this balance.

Unlike Ross, Brimelow sees no grotesque bodies. Inflammatory racial figures occasionally break through his discursive *sang-froid* – he refers, for example, to an INS waiting room that is 'teeming' with people who are 'almost entirely colored'[20] – but operating within the modern episteme, inflected by the displacement of subjective perception by technologies of data collection, Brimelow relies on the self-evidence of his data displays rather than his senses. America's 'good looks'[21] are not so much threatened as the numerical domination of white Americans. He constructs a graph showing the projected increase of the population (if current rates of immigration continue). The threat to America's whiteness is figuratively rather than discursively represented, for the graph is in the form of a black wedge on top of a gray area, representing normal growth.[22] He also constructs a graph with a 'pincer shape' (again with black colour growing larger), representing the extent to which Asian, Hispanic, and non-Spanish blacks are squeezing out the white majority.[23] Reflective of his quest to achieve epistemic authority for his version of nativism, the graphs are included in a section entitled 'truth'.

If we employ imagery with more historical depth, the resulting temporal trajectory can connect Ross and Brimelow to the prophetic tradition. Although separated by a half century and operating within different epistemes, they are both Jeremiahs, who bear a striking resemblance to the original; they issue dire warnings about a national catastrophe. Moreover, their Jeremiads can be usefully contrasted with a narrative based on the political economy of migration. It has been clear for centuries that a combination of political and economic forces are primarily implicated in creating the flows of people from one to another global location, and the twentieth century flows are no exception. They can be understood in terms of the demands of commercial producers and the collaboration of governments, which, in varying degrees, comply with those demands. The significant actors – capitalist enterprises and migrating workers – function within a larger structural imperative of modernity, the process of decolonization, which, in Balibar's terms, has created a 'new political space'. It is, he notes,

> not merely a space in which strategies are formed, and capital technologies and messages circulate, but a space in which entire populations subject to the law of the market come into contact physically and symbolically.[24]

Ignoring this larger structural dynamic, Ross and Brimelow both pick up the story at the level of contact. Reaching into the past to imagine its genesis, the story of migration they tell is more biographical than structural. Their lens has no depth of focus; it features individual actors. Specifically, they construct immigration as a series of perversely motivated, individual decisions. Romanticizing the earlier, northern European immigrants, for example, Ross describes them as 'home seekers' in contrast with the latter flows of more 'common stock', for example, Italians, who come as 'job hunters'. It is greed that brings *them* to America.[25]

Brimelow has a similarly romantic view of what he calls 'colonial stock Americans,' (they get to be 'Americans' as soon as they hit the shore) who 'had things rolling along pretty well before mass immigration began'.[26] And he specifically argues that current immigration 'does not seem to be affected very much by the economic conditions in the United States'.[27] His preferred model of the influx is permissive US immigration policy as the enabling condition and economic greed as the immigrant motivation, implying that destination USA is a result of 'alien' decision making: 'Whether these foreigners deign to come and make their claim on America – and on the American taxpayer – is pretty much up to them.'[28]

The convenient neglect of political economy in Ross's case was noted in Horace Kallen's review shortly after the publication of Ross's 1914 book. Referring to Gary, Lawrence, Chicago, and Pittsburgh as 'industrial camps of foreign mercenaries',[29] Kallen located the immigration issue squarely in the domain of political economy. The greed of the entrepreneur, coupled with the 'indifference of government,' he argued, 'displaced the high demanding labor by cheaper labor'. Allowing greed to set the standard, government has been subordinated to the 'service of wealth'.[30]

Although his model of the relationship between enterprise and government was simplistic, Kallen's identification of the cheap labour demands of entrepreneurs, provoked by changes in global economic structures, remains a cogent explanation for the 'illegal alien' composition of today's workforce. What he discerned in the early part of this century remains the case. Anti-immigrant sentiments continue to obscure the structurally induced complicity between entrepreneurs and government. While, for example, the US Senate appeared to be responding to a national hysteria about illegal 'aliens' when they passed the 'Immigration and Financial Responsibility Act of 1996', Wade Graham is undoubtedly correct in his assessment that it was never meant to significantly alter illegal immigration.[31] As he notes, 'Mexicans will continue to go where jobs *are* being created for them, and that will mean crossing the border,'[32] and that illegal immigration is only epiphenomenally a law-enforcement event; 'it is fundamentally a labor market event'.[33] Senators recognize, he argues, that a serious attempt to close the border is a bad career move since 'no small number of them owe their seats to the patronage of right-wing manufacturing and agribusiness interests desirous of nothing so much as low minimum wage and unfettered access to cheap non-union labor from the Third World'.[34]

How then should we understand the rhetoric of government which, more or less in a bipartisan chorus, laments the presence of the illegal immigrant? Historically, governments have engaged in a politics of representation aimed at legitimating the nation as a national culture distinct from other nations. The forces behind the shaping of a cultural nationalism throughout the nineteenth and early twentieth centuries were occasioned in part by a desire to create a nationally manageable workforce. Among other things, this required state initiatives to reshape the older, traditional affiliations of clan and family. Increasingly, the family became subjected to official intervention, aimed at the biopolitical control of the population.[35] The state's politics of representation – its claim to house a coherent national culture – was accompanied by a series of policy initiatives aimed at imposing that coherence. However, in the current condition of a more global economy, which produces an internationally migrating workforce, the state is in an ideational bind. It has to live with an anachronistic form of nationalism that its politics of representation often reasserts at the same time that it attenuates that nationalism with its economic policies.

While their representational practices have kept 'foreign populations' at a distance conceptually, other practices of industrially and economically advanced states have produced flows of such peoples across state boundaries. Powerful interests within states seeking to attract workers create pressures to relax immigration controls. The flows in turn provoke expressions of cultural anxiety over the changing character of the domestic ethnoscape as well as concern over competition for jobs. Groups articulating such worries exert pressures through their governmental representatives to tighten controls over immigration, and local and state politicians run successful campaigns that pander to cultural anxieties.

At the level of official discourse, the state responds positively to such demands for tightening while, at the level of economic policy, it encourages the border transgressing flows and relaxation of controls. Roxanne Doty has characterized the contradiction as a form of double writing. At the level of representation, she argues, the state constructs itself as an autonomous geo-political unity, and its society as 'an a priori historical presence'.[36] In effect, it engages in a pedagogy that constructs the 'givenness of its social, geo-political, and economic space';[37] it continually represents its social spaces as naturally distinct. But at the level of its economic functioning, the state encourages flows that contest 'the givenness of social space'.[38] And because this encouragement constitutes a threat to the state's territorialized identity, statecraft, at the level of the story it tells about itself, is duplicitous: it consists of a kind of *double-writing* that draws upon the authority of the pedagogical and simultaneously engages in a performative function of social representation whereby the inside is continually reproduced and its articulation with the outside concealed.[39]

This tension between the pedagogical, 'the space of the given',[40] and the performative, 'the space of that which must be constructed',[41] is made manifest over the issue of immigration. The stories through which the state reproduces its coherence, its imagined culture coherence and social unity, fail to acknowledge both the permeability of its borders that its functioning encourages and the internal modes of cultural diversity and ambiguity that challenge its pedagogy of unity.

It is this 'pedagogy of unity' that has been primary in the vociferations of Jeremiahs, and it constitutes the organizing principle of both Ross's and Brimelow's constructions of the 'America' threatened by immigration flows. Jeremiahs predicate their concerns on a story, a narration of the nation within which some founding acts, purposive in-migrations, and historical continuities have forged a culturally unified national people, whose integrity as a 'people' is threatened by the nature of the different and newer in-migrations against which they sound their respective alarms. A challenge to the exclusionary practice they advocate must therefore come from a challenge to the national stories on which they rely.

To launch that challenge it is necessary to stage some juxtapositions that deepen an appreciation of the significance of narrating the nation for constructing the "alien" threat. Accordingly, the scene of writing shifts to compare past and present identity tales in Israel and the United States.

Tales of Peoples, Tales of States

Increasingly, the more critical genres of social theory locate much of the basis for a nation's coherence in its identity stories. In these approaches, a nation's unity-promoting articulations are treated not simply as ideological expressions, oriented towards supporting a particular apparatus of state power. Nor are they treated, at the other end of the sovereignty code, as manifestations of the people's will. Instead, they are conceived in a language that registers interpretive contentions between the legitimations of mainstream national culture and what Homi Bhabha refers to as 'those easily obscured, but highly significant recesses of the national culture from which alternative constituencies of peoples and oppositional analytic capacities may emerge' . . .[42]

Given the complex sets of forces that have been responsible both for assembling as a 'people' those groupings identified as 'nations' and the ambiguities and contentiousness associated with the ways that such assemblages claim territories, their primary national stories must bear considerable weight. Indeed, there are nothing other than commitments to stories for a national people to give themselves a historical trajectory that testifies to their collective coherence. In modern states, the tendency is 'for collective identities to be cast as national histories in the support of claims to independent statehood'.[43] Although Brimelow supports this casting, asserting that, 'a nation is the interlacing of ethnicity and culture. And a nation-state is its political expression,'[44] it is the case, rather, that 'no nation, that is no national state', as Balibar has noted, 'has an ethnic basis . . . but they do have to institute in real (and therefore in historical) time their imaginary unity *against* other possible unities.'[45]

The continuous process of constructing affiliations, necessary to reproduce a coherent national imaginary, produces a mythic connection between nationhood and personhood in the form of a story of how the nation arises naturally from the character of its people. The maintenance of such myths requires control over discourse in general and over the dominant story of national origin in particular, for many identity claims, expressed within national societies, do not aid and abet the coherence project of the state; often, they 'are claims against the modern governmentality altogether'.[46]

Among the strategies of discursive containment employed to maintain the myth of a cultural nation is what Michel Foucault has called the 'commentary', the invocation of historical texts or the words of exemplary authors for purposes of re-enacting the terms of one's collective coherence. The commentary, he states:

> is governed by a dream of repetition in disguise: at its horizon there is perhaps nothing but what was at its point of departure – mere recitation. Commentary exorcizes the chance element in discourse by giving it its due; it allows us to say something other than the text itself, but on condition that it is the text itself which is said, and in a sense completed.[47]

Commentaries, which attempt to contain disruptions to legitimating stories, are of course countered by alternative narratives or even subversive readings of the same texts. And the dynamics of disruption and containment, as well as the accompanying cultural anxieties and struggles, occupy much of the analysis to follow. However, to provide a frame to treat such contentions, it is necessary to bring into focus the vagaries involved in the production and maintenance of national stories. Most significantly, the stories must create boundaries between a people and its others and, at the same time, legitimate the basis for the territorialization of its collective identity.[48] They must impose a model of identity/difference, administer silences, and over-code recalcitrant experiences inasmuch as there is no ultimately stable basis for such collective uniqueness. All national stories incorporate such discursive economies of identity, but here the focus is on two cases: Israel and the United States. With respect to the former, an appreciation of the nation-state story must begin with the story of the ancient Israelites. With respect to the latter, it is necessary to trace a trajectory from colonial to contemporary America.

Turning first to the situation of ancient Israel, we can begin with the biblical injunction that continues to influence the mythic territory known as 'the land of Israel'. In Genesis 17:8 it is reported that Jehovah said, 'And I will give unto thee, to thy seed after thee the land wherein thou art a stranger, all the land of Canaan, for an everlasting possession.' This divine land grant, the biblical promise by Jehovah to Abraham, has had a variety of consequences for Jewish–other relations throughout history, but most significantly for purposes of this analysis, it resulted in a paradox in the midst of the primary identity story of the Jewish people. This paradox is at the centre of an 'Old

Testament' reading by Edmund Leach, an elaborate exercise of Levi-Strauss's method of structural interpretation.[49]

Leach focuses on a contradiction that has plagued Jewish history 'from the earliest times right down to the present day':

> On the one hand the practice of sectarian endogamy is essential to maintain the purity of the faith, on the other hand exogamous marriages may be politically expedient if peaceful relations are to be maintained with hostile neighbors.[50]

This tension is revealed in the biblical texts, which 'consistently affirm the righteousness of endogamy and the sinfulness of exogamy',[51] but nevertheless have those in the main genealogical line, from Judah onwards, taking foreign wives. Because of the political pressure on the texts to conform to 'the doctrine of the unique legitimacy of the royal house of Judah and the unitary ascendency of Solomon and Jerusalem',[52] the marriages are treated as within-tribe, legitimate ones. For example, although both Tamar and Ruth are not Israelites, and although their couplings with members of the Israelite lineage (Judah and Boaz respectively) are the seductions of women treated in the text as harlots (the former explicitly and the latter implicitly), the descendants are treated as pure-blooded. [53]

What emerges from Leach's reading is a mythic story that has been arranged both to legitimate Jewish title to the 'land of Canaan' and to affirm the historical coherence of the Jewish people. Yet the story achieves this coherence by turning what is arbitrary and radically contingent into something historically destined and expected. Jewish identity through the centuries is constituted as a commitment to a continuous genealogical and spatial story.

Despite the persistence of this mythic story, historical investigations reveal that the 'the Jewish people' is more the result of cultural amalgamation than one of ethnic and cultural exclusivity. While the biblical story is more or less a story of 'how one man, through the generations, gradually becomes a whole nation',[54] it is clear that such patriarchal stories are legends belied by the findings of ethnohistory.[55] In the light of the latter it has been shown that the ancient Israelites coalesced in various ways – economically, legally, and linguistically, in addition to intermarriage – with Canaanite tribes. Under the influence of Canaanite practices, they changed from nomadic herders to fixed-dwelling agriculturalists.[56]

Canaanites and other resident-immigrants in the Israelite territory remained ambiguously understood neighbours. They were objects of both moral solicitude, in the form of injunctions of tolerance and special protections, and cultural dangers.[57] Some of Deuteronomy (as well as Exodus, Judges, and the Book of the Covenant) is devoted to the need to protect the alien from oppression,[58] while some of Deuteronomy is also devoted to demands from priestly authorities to 'liberate Israel from Canaanite customs' and 'to protect the Israelite community against Canaanite influence'.[59] Interestingly, however, the legal structures invoked to protect the purity of the Israelitic culture were markedly Canaanite in origin.

One could refer to the irony of using Canaanite legalities, assimilated to the Israelite codes, to distance the Israelite cult from Canaanisms, but the more appropriate conceptual trope is deconstructive. Put simply, the norms with which the ancient Israelites sought to expel otherness from its cultural midst relied precisely on the culture of that otherness.[60] During the cultural encounter, the tent-dwelling, herding, tribal society of the Israelites mingled with a city-dwelling, monarchical group of Canaanites, and city practices ultimately dominated the resulting legal infrastructure of Israelite codes. Deuteronomy is primarily a reflection of municipal law.[61] References, for example, to the authority of 'The Elders at the gate' had supplanted the authority of clan patriarchs. 'We can only conclude', Johannes Pederson asserts, 'that the Laws of Deuteronomy and the Book of the Covenant are almost thoroughly Canaanite'.[62]

Nevertheless, a parallel priestly tradition shadowed the process of acculturation, reacting against Canaanite influence and exerting continual pressure to separate, as much as possible, the Israelitic cult from Canaanism. The ancient Israelites had not only developed a significant Canaanite psyche[63] but had also taken over many of the Canaanite spiritual practices, ranging from the conceptual: ideas of 'man' and nature, to the ritual: the infusion of sexual and drinking rites into worship practices.[64]

It was precisely the Israelitic practising of Canaanite rituals that animated the prophetic tradition. Jeremiah in particular had harsh words about the sexual, drinking cults of the Baal worshipers, those whom, he claimed, have 'assembled themselves by troops in harlots' houses' (Jeremiah 5:7). But most significantly, the prophetic tradition reflects the struggle of elements within the Israelitic cult to protect not simply particular modes of spirituality but rather the ethnic and political boundaries of the people.

On the one hand, there was the crisis created by exogenous powers: 'the prophets could not have emerged', notes Max Weber, 'except for the world politics of the great powers',[65] namely the threat of conquest by Egyptians, Assyrians, and Babylonians. On the other hand, the foreign threat was heightened, according to the prophets, by the anger of Yahweh in reaction to the assimilative practices of the Israelites. Then, as now (in contemporary state societies), there was an entanglement between the map of external danger and domestic intercultural antagonisms. Domestically, the prophets' laments were, in Weber's terms, 'gratuitous'.[66] Unlike Egyptian and Hellenic prophets, who were in effect house oracles, the Hebrew prophets were independent alarmists. Their preachments of doom reflected not only a heightened and anachronistic mode of piety but also spatial history.

For the prophets 'the desert times remained . . . the truly pious epoch'.[67] They lamented the demise of a desert existence, for in the encounter between attacking desert clans and city-dwelling residents, the resulting assimilation produced a cultural hybridity that favoured the city life and monarchical structures of the Canaanites. Under the influence of city life many Israelites absorbed Canaanite spiritual practices. The Canaanite remained a foreigner within the Israelite governance in both pre- and post-monarchical Israel, but the Israelites became significantly Canaanized.

The spatial structure of the ancient Israelites affected the way in which the alien-other, both the Canaanites who were alien residents and the 'foreigners', members of other tribes, were objects of the Deuteronomic laws. The Canaanite resident-immigrants were recognized as 'more or less permanently part of the Israelite tribal community'.[68] Before the development of the Israelite monarchy, the approach to the foreigner was based not on a national consciousness – there was no single, centralized state – but on a clan consciousness. Since there were several Israelite tribes, the Israelite unity was constituted as a spatial dispersion, best viewed as a series of overlapping circles rather than as a concentrically organized nation. The foreigner within could not therefore be construed as a threat to a national, political unity. And because the Israelitic cult was a lineage system rather than a nation-state, foreigners were assimilated through intermarriage not through a process of entry into citizenship. Their presence could not be a threat to an imaginary, the nation-state, which did not exist. Moreover, even in the case of the non-assimilated foreigner, an injunction referring back to the Israelites' Egyptian bondage – 'for you were aliens in Egypt' (Exodus 22:24, 23:9) – encouraged a treatment of them as vulnerable foreigners. [69] In addition, given the absence of a unified national imaginary, the foreigner was always constructed as an individual, not as part of another people. Insofar as there were generalities, mention was made of *vulnerable* types: widows, orphans, and foreigners.

This 'alien' problematic in ancient Israel provides an important background for understanding the politics of constructing the foreigner and immigrant threat in the contemporary state of Israel. First, the ethno-historical trajectory disrupts the identity story of the Jewish people which aims at producing a clear title to 'the land of Israel' for an unambiguously continuous 'people.' The 'alien-other' haunts the story of that 'people' producing an impetus to repress more strongly aspects of internal difference. And, second, the nature of the spatial history, which produced a hybrid nation out of an amalgam of desert herders and patriarchs on the one hand and city-dwelling agriculturalists and monarchists on the other, provides a contrast to the contemporary structures behind the motivational injunctions surrounding the construction of the 'alien-other'.

The modern Israeli state exists in an ideational climate that exerts more pressure on reducing cultural pluralism than was the case in ancient Israel. Precisely because it is a modern state, Israel partakes of the contemporary nationalist psyche (it shares with other contemporary 'nation-states'), which manifests a reticence to tolerate a multinational or multiethnic basis.[70] And, more specifically, as a diasporic state whose population has grown rapidly since independence – it tripled for example from 1948 to 1961 – Israel has concentrated heavily on producing an official version of its immediate nation-building past, a more or less Zionist history.[71] In addition to providing a model of contemporary Israeli history, Zionism carries with it an injunction that effectively represses cultural pluralism; it is the motivating slogan, 'a land without people for a people without a land" This injunction perpetuates the myth that the Arab population of Israel was never really there.[72]

Yet the state of Israel does not wholly deny the legitimate presence of its Arab population. Arabs are variously situated within two decisively different modalities within which 'Israel' has been constructed. The state of Israel officially permits Arabs to be citizens, but the Zionist-inspired 'land of Israel' (*Eretz Israel*), a place existing in a legendary narrative that reaches back to Yahweh's land grant to Abraham, constitutes Arabs as 'non-Jews,' and as 'strangers in our midst'.[73] The contradiction imposed on the Arab within is therefore a matter of two different spatial and ethnic stories.

To what extent can Arabs be regarded as 'strangers' to Jews? As the ethno-historical work on ancient Israel shows, it is problematic to speak of Jews as *a* people, and the issue becomes more complex when the trajectory of that 'people' is followed through the Diaspora. If we allow the collectivity assembled as 'the Jews' to represent themselves as unitary historical actors, our analytic abdicates control. The time of the Jews looks different when the motion through time and space operates under a critical direction. Cutting to the present, for example, we can note that the installation of Hebrew as a national language of Israel functions as a symbol of common cultural heritage, but a move back to a longer historical angle of vision indicates that Hebrew has not been a historical mechanism of cultural distinction for a 'Jewish people' as a whole. During the process of acculturation in ancient Israel, the Israelites' vernacular language became Aramaic. The linguistic evidence pertaining to ancient Israel/Palestine suggests 'that Jews, like almost all other national and tribal groups in the Levant and Mesopotamia, generally came to adopt Aramaic as their normal means of communication'[74] Hebrew remained an important symbol of Jewish distinctiveness – by the third century BCE it was used on coins, and the curatorial class associated with the temple and Torah used it to distinguish themselves from the rest of the population – but throughout the Diaspora, a temple-based, curatorial tradition was not strong. [75]

Significantly, the ancient Israelites did not consider a shared language as an important way of distinguishing themselves from their neighbours, even though they often thought of themselves as a distinct nation. The speaking of Hebrew was not, in sum, an essential element of ancient Jewish identity. It was, then as later during the Diaspora, more of a 'social marker used to distinguish the protectors of the Torah from other classes',[76] Moreover, even the language of the Torah, which was protected, has not been based on a wholly separate or purely Hebrew language. The Hebrew Bible has evolved on the basis of what Hebrew shares with other Semitic languages. Throughout the history of the 'Hebrew Bible', emendations have resulted from philological work in which the meanings of Hebrew words and phrases have been changed by examining the terms and expressions in cognate Semitic languages (as well as others): Aramaic, Classical Syriac, Accadian, Ugaritic, and Classical Arabic.[77]

Ironically, Arabs were not only already there in the supposed 'land without people' of the Zionist imaginary but have been always already there in the supposed language of Jewish distinction, Hebrew. For example, one resolution of a disputed passage in the Book of Judges, which had long been considered difficult and ambiguous, was achieved with attention to a relevant Arabic verb.[78]

In addition to the historical evidence of shared Canaanite–Israelite and Arab–Jewish cultural productions, the social logic of identity politics frustrates any attempt to draw a firm identity boundary between Jew and Arab. A drive towards exclusivity always draws a people ever closer to its other(s), to those who serve to help the 'people' recognize itself as a separate whole. Accordingly, in the modern period, the Israeli-Jewish society 'has been connected with the Arab as if he were its Siamese Twin'.[79] The Arab, 'the figure expelled from the camp', has held 'the key to the identity' of the Jew'.[80] And because the identity economy of sameness/difference with which Israeli nationalism has tried to produce claims for exclusivity contains unreconcilable ambiguities, the claim to distinctiveness has required an energetic denial of otherness within.

Nevertheless, while the identity dependence of the Jew on the Arab has been denied at the level of official discourse, various forms of cultural expression in contemporary Israel have challenged a model that asserts an unproblematic exclusivity for Israeli–Jewish identity.[81] The problematic that Leach discloses in the Hebrew Bible has therefore persisted. The production of identity coherence and exclusivity continues to be a matter of how a people's story is told.

In the 1990s Ammiel Alcalay has made a concerted effort to disrupt the dominant identity story of the state of Israel. He has explored the historical depth of the Arab–Jewish cultural imbrication, the persistence of Levantine culture, which militates against the official Israeli policy of a Jewish state and an end to the Diaspora, and the desire to locate the Arab outside the boundaries of the Israeli polity. Alcalay treats both the well-known divisions in Israeli society between European and 'Oriental' Jews and, more importantly, the affinity of the Oriental Jew to Arab culture. The reconstruction of ancient Hebrew as a modern national language in Israel has constituted a meaning system aimed, among other things, at expunging the Levantine – shared Arab–Jewish – cultural system that had developed since the period of Islamic domination of Spain and the Middle East, a period during which Jewish culture developed within an Islamic context.

Alcalay shows how Hebrew, along with other systems of articulation, has imposed an order of truth of identity congenial to a project of national unification, Jewish exclusiveness, and Euro-Jewish dominance. It is a project of national coherence that requires the Arab as an absolute other. But this symbolic boundary-drawing, which has accompanied policies of actual spatial partition, and has been supported by complicit discourses within official, popular, and academic venues, must confront strong evidence of Arabness within. The Oriental Jew retains strong connections with Arab culture. It is not unusual, for example, for an Israeli Jew from Iraq to recognize her- or himself better in Palestinian poetry than in the contemporary Hebrew novel. [82]

The dominant cultural unity story of the state of Israel, however, retains its privilege, repressing recalcitrant elements of unfinished national assimilation, even as the ethno-historical evidence indicates that there was never a unity except by dint of a unifying mythology that repressed elements of difference. The repression of acculturation, which constituted the ancient Israelite as a historical character, is required to the extent that the official Israeli discourse strives to reconstitute the Israeli Jew as a unique and unalloyed national character.

The problem of Arab otherness is accompanied by a problem of Jewish otherness. In the state of Israel, there is more than one Jewish character. One of the dominant characters emerges from what might best be termed the frontier story of nation-building in contemporary Israel. Controversial, but still significant, is what is popularly known as the 'Tower and Stockade' story.[83] Constructed in part to counter the traditional story of the passivity of the exilic Jew, it 'serves as a culturally compelling "foundation myth" ', valorizing heroic acts of settlement in defiance of 'the antagonistic policy of the British mandate and armed attacks of Arab gangs'.[84]

Although there is significant resistance to the story as a narrative of Israeli identity, it serves to energize the continuing settlement process into disputed territories. Moreover, it allocates a privileged social and political identity to original settlers, who are primarily European in background, while de-privileging more recent immigrants: holocaust survivors and other recent political refugees from both the old Soviet Union and Arab countries. Given the dominant, Euro-oriented story of Israel's nation-building, the more recent influx of immigrants is read as a cultural threat, augmenting the number of perpetual strangers in the land. 'Oriental' Jews, for example, take on the 'alien' status of the domestic Arabs.

The new immigrants place specific pressures on Israel's attempt to construct a unified national history. The struggles of new immigrants for significant identity recognition, especially by 'Oriental Jews', has been reflected in controversies over school history texts. Although the curriculum, which from the 1950s onwards credited European Jews almost exclusively with the founding of the nation, continues to represent this as the primary national story, there is more emphasis on the cultural pluralism of Israeli society.[85] Most significantly, the dominance of the pioneering, Euro-Jewish settler over various Arab and Jewish others in Israel is maintained only to the degree that the story of violence at the frontiers remains the primary national story. This story turns domestic Arabs (citizens and foreign workers) into both immediate security threats and into 'demographic' threats, that is, threats to the construction of Israel as a Jewish state.[86] And the 'demographic threat' is also associated with the burgeoning population of non-Arab, imported workers.[87] But most of the contention generated by the story at present arises from the way it turns Soviet and 'Oriental' Jews into cultural threats whose assimilation into a Western civilizational model is required to maintain the unity of Israel as a nation.[88]

In many ways, the narrative contentions and repressions characterizing Israeli nationhood, from ancient times to the present, display striking similarities with the problem of producing a culturally unified American nation and with the cultural anxieties articulated along the way. Not the least of the points of comparison is the similarity in the frontier narrative of the modern Israeli state with the legendary American story, exemplified in the title of Theodore Roosevelt's frontier story in his *The Winning of the West* (1889). However, a cogent comparison must begin with a flashback to a period well before Roosevelt helps to contribute to America's cultural mythologies.

Constituting America

The drive to constitute 'American' identity, like the process in Israel, has expressed itself with both repressions and contentions. As Myra Jehlen has shown, the dominant founding story is one of making a civilization out of nature.[89] The American story is, in this respect, very close to that of the ancient Israelites inasmuch as it is a story of leaving unruly nature (a wilderness) behind and establishing a stable, law-abiding national space. Of course 'wilderness', as it has been evoked in both cases, has a deeply religious connotation. It is a place where divine sanction has yet to be fulfilled. The divine sanction scenario, upon which both Israeli and American national stories draw, serves also to diminish ethical reflection on the fate of the peoples displaced by the process through which the conquering peoples fulfill their destinies.

For example, in a reaction to Michael Walzer's contemporary celebration of the mythic version of ancient Israelite conquest, Edward Said has juxtaposed a view from the vantage point of the Canaanite/other. In his review of *Exodus and Revolution* (1985), Said reminds us of Walzer's 'violence of representation'[90] by providing what he calls a 'Canaanite view' of the *Exodus*; he effectively identifies the scarcity of the moral solicitude in Walzer's story, which is not only a moral tale – specifically a redemption story – but also a nationalist one. Canaanites cannot ultimately be objects of political recognition or moral concern because Walzer's affirmation of a nationalist political geography is also a moral geography.[91] Jewish control over the state of Israel is part of the redemption story, and Walzer 'minimizes . . . a sense of responsibility for what a people undergoing redemption does to other less fortunate people, unredeemed, strange, displaced and outside moral concern'.[92]

The dominant American founding story, animated by a morally sanctioned mission, is also insensitive to the fates of those displaced. 'Americans saw themselves as building their civilization out of nature itself, as neither the analogue nor the translation of Natural Law but its direct expression.'[93] The myth of the vacancy of the place of settlement governed the story, for the 'wilderness' was regarded as effectively unoccupied as European settlers saw themselves as 'quickening a virgin land'.[94]

There are additional parallels between the legendary story of ancient Israel and the legendary versions of the American founding. Sacvan Bercovitch's investigation of Puritan ideologies and genres of discourse, for example, reveals that like the ancient Israelites, the Puritans saw themselves as having entered into a covenant. Governor Winthrop explicitly invoked, 'the ominous precedent of Israel'.[95] America was to be the new Canaan, enjoying the positive land grant from God, who, according to Winthrop, had pledged 'to protect, assist, and favor them above any other community on earth'.[96] In addition to the covenant model and the legendary notion of God's land grant to the Puritans, a new chosen people, a variety of historical narrations have constituted America's legendary version of its history. For present purposes, however, the cultural encounter with Native Americans (the legendary version's 'Indians'), in which, ironically, the earlier residents, like ancient Israel's Canaanites, were constituted as strangers in the land, provides a focus for an Israel–America comparison.

The Puritans thought of themselves as 'chosen' in a way that coincides with the western expansion of the Euro-American settlers. Their movement across what they regarded as a 'wilderness' was a sacred 'errand' according to Samuel Danforth, a seventeenth-century American Jeremiah.[97] It was a required movement from a degenerate civilization to the purity of a wilderness situation. Reminiscent of the demand of the biblical Jeremiah, Danforth's injunction was part of his sacred mission to remind the colonists that their afflictions were visited by a God angered by their failure to recall their errand.[98] Whatever the effect of such injunctions – doubtless they simply supplied a legitimating rationale and a fragment of a legendary history that accompanied more economically predatory aims – they remain part of a mythologizing of an 'America' consolidated ideationally as well as spatially by its westward expansion.

While the seventeenth-century expansion continued under the supposition that the colonists had inherited the mantel of the ancient Israelites,[99] by the eighteenth century more regionally developed stories displaced the biblical version of America's expansion.[100] The significant icons were no longer virtuous, self-sacrificing Puritans but heroic adventurers and Indian fighters. Summarizing this shift, Richard Slotkin notes that 'in the American mythogenesis the founding fathers were not those eighteenth century gentlemen who composed a nation at Philadelphia. Rather, they were those who . . . tore violently a nation from the implacable and opulent wilderness – the rogues, adventurers, and land-boomers; the Indian fighters, traders, missionaries, explorers, and hunters who killed and were killed until they had mastered the wilderness.'[101]

Accordingly, cultural heroes such as Daniel Boone, a lover of the wilderness and an exemplar of one who achieved sacred cult status through acts of violence, became ideal Americans attaching the national identity to its violent western movement. Significantly these national heroes were developed in connection with a cultural anxiety over what it should mean to be 'American'. The anxieties were expressed as the need to build a story of Americans that radically excluded others from the cast of national characters. The legend of the violent winning of the West, a story that focuses mainly on accounts of the Indian wars, constituted a playing-out of the colonist's more general cultural anxieties.[102] This is evident in the way the violence of the Indian wars were legitimated by accompanying accounts of radical difference between Euro- and Native Americans, for example, emphases on different approaches to land tenure in which Indians did not have a legitimate model of possession,[103] and models of character in which Indians were constructed as expressive rather than control- ling in their impulses.[104]

Subsequent responses to cultural anxieties have often taken the form of repeating the story of the winning of the west; the retelling of the myth of violent (yet sacred) expansion has been a dominant mode through which 'America' has performed its legendary national iden- tity. Such textual performances, in which Americans are constituted (or reconstituted) in response to cultural anxieties about appropriate personhood, have been evident in various historical periods, but one in particular, in which America's mythic western past was reaffirmed, is especially pertinent to the politics of constructing the 'alien-other'.

Theodore Roosevelt's gloss on 'the winning of the West' was written during a period in which the boundaries of the working body were being extended. Specifically, Roosevelt's role in attempting to author American nationhood and personhood is associated with a crisis of masculinity at the turn of this century. As the industrial age increasingly lent mechanical extensions to the working body, there were expressions of concern about the depletion of masculinity. Such significant cultural actors as Thompson Seton, a co-founder of the scouting movement, concerned themselves during this period with the craft of making men as an 'antidote to anxieties about the *depletion* of agency and virility in consumer and machine culture'.[105] As it is put in the first *Boy Scouts of America* handbook, it is necessary 'to combat the system that has turned such a large proportion of our robust, manly, self-reliant boyhood into a lot of flat-chested cigarette smo- kers, with shaky nerves and doubtful vitality'.[106] The anxieties ex- pressed at the time were organized around a confusion of agency, as 'men' enacted their work with the increasing aid of mechanical prostheses which, on the one hand, extended bodily capacities but, on the other, ambiguated issues of agency and value. Telling the American story as the story of the 'winning of the West' was among Roosevelt's solutions to what he saw as a crisis in nationhood and national personhood.

Not surprisingly various nationalist, anti-immigration Jeremiahs have invoked Roosevelt's mythic treatment of the Euro-American movement westward. Brimelow does so explicitly; his commentary invokes Roosevelt's mythologizing as if it were an ethno-historical investigation that traces a 'perfectly continuous history' of Anglo-

Saxon settlement.[107] Brimelow's purpose is to argue that as regards important nation-building epochs, 'America' has been effectively ethnically homogeneous; the westward settlement of English-speaking people, he avers, quoting Roosevelt without criticism, was 'the crowning and greatest achievement', having made America part of the 'heritage of the dominant world races'.[108] Thus, for Brimelow, the threat of non-whites and non-English speakers is to a cultural homogeneity seemingly established by the Rooseveltian fable.[109]

Ross also worried about the 'loss of political like-mindedness' engendered by the addition of immigrants, but for him the primary threat was to the American bloodlines, which he imagined had been created by the rigors of the western adventure ('The blood now being injected into the veins of our people is "sub-common" ').[110] Thus, for example, he thought that Jews make poor Americans because they are not fit to haul canoes through the wilderness:

> On the physical side the Hebrews are the polar opposite of our pioneer breed . . . it will be long before they produce the stoical type who blithely fares forth into the wilderness, portaging his canoe, poling it against the current, wading in the torrents, living on bacon and beans, and sleeping on the ground, all for 'fun' or 'to keep hard'.[111]

Roosevelt's *Winning of the West* (1889) certainly supports the inferences of these two differently situated but exemplary immigration alarmists, but there is another element of his legendary history that bears scrutiny. There is a remarkable disjuncture in Roosevelt's text, a telling economy of 'Indian' presence and absence in the West. Constructed in part as a spatial history, Roosevelt's fable depopulates the western landscape. Reminiscent of the Zionist reference to Palestine as a 'land without people' is Roosevelt's reference to the Native American-occupied west as part of 'the world's waste spaces'.[112] Insofar as 'Indians' had a significant presence during the 'spread of the English-speaking peoples', it was only as occasional visitors:

> The white settler has merely moved into an uninhabited waste; he does not feel that he is committing a wrong, for he knows perfectly well that the land is really owned by no one. It is never even visited, except perhaps for a week or two every year.[113]

However, in the places where Roosevelt's analysis becomes an ethno-history (albeit a legendary one), the West becomes repopulated with 'savage and formidable foes',[114] against whom 'the English race' maintains its integrity by driving them off or exterminating them rather than, like the Spanish in other colonial venues, 'sitting down in their midst' and becoming a 'mixed race'.[115] In its pseudo, ethno-historical moments, *The Winning of the West* is a romantic *soldat-esque* in which brave pioneers fight their way westward, impeded at every step by the Indians' 'fierce and dogged resistance'[116] until they gain what is rightfully theirs. But, when justice becomes the focus in the text – 'the settler and pioneer have at bottom had justice on their side'[117] – the 'fierce and dogged' foes again disappear, and what has been conquered turns out to have been merely 'nothing but a game preserve for squalid savages'.[118]

The economy of presence and absence for Native Americans in Roosevelt's text, produced at the end of the nineteenth century, is evident in the historical production of American civics and history texts throughout the past two centuries. Reflecting Roosevelt's pseudo ethno-history and his concern with Americanization, civics texts from the early part of the twentieth century emphasized Anglo-Saxon accomplishments, devoting, for example, more space to Sir Francis Drake than to Spanish 'discoverers' and concentrating on English rather than French colonists.[119] And, not surprisingly, the 'rediscovery' of Anglo Saxon roots in the texts coincided with a significant influx of non-English immigrants.[120]

By contrast, in the early nineteenth century, when there was less cultural anxiety about the constitution of Americans, the civics texts in the 1830s and 1840s represented 'North American Indians' as important people despite their not being Christians.[121] Later in the nineteenth century, however, they become 'savage, barbarous and half-civilized',[122] and as the Anglo-Saxon revival in the texts proceeds in the early twentieth century, they become lazy and child-like until they disappear in the 1930s, not to return until the 1960s as 'ethnics' and the 1970s as objects of official policy.[123]

Ethno-historical Challenges

Roosevelt's drama of the English-speaking people versus the 'squalid savages' deserves further scrutiny, not only because it has been appropriated in Brimelow's anti-immigration tract but also because it is radically contradicted by both the history of 'English-speaking peoples' and the history of the Euro-Native American encounter in the west. Resisting Roosevelt's implied chronology, we can substitute a historical montage, turning first of all to the period that received most of Roosevelt's attention. The 'English' spoken by these people who supposedly won the West was not a cultural property that divided the

Anglo-Saxons from other peoples. Indeed, the history of English, like the history of a 'people', is a history of acculturation and co-invention. What Roosevelt called a perfectly continuous history of English-speaking people looks discontinuous, interculturally provoked, and often accidental and arbitrary from the point of view of the articulate noises they have made.

What has been historically produced as 'English' is not only the product of dialects brought to England by Jutes, Saxons, and Angles but also the languages of Romans, Scandinavians and Celts, in an earlier period[124] and French in a later period.[125] The history of English in England is a history of the linguistic amalgamations following invasions and other cultural encounters. Without going into an elaborate philological analysis, a focus on the various episodes of the Latinization of English is telling. Three historical epochs are primarily involved. First was the Roman conquest, which brought classical Latin into the language mix in Britain, then the spread of Christianity, which infused medieval Latin into English, and then the development of Renaissance science, which added significantly more Latin to English.[126]

The story of what H. L. Mencken called 'the American language' is similarly telling.[127] What Roosevelt called a perfectly continuous history of English speakers was more aptly described by Mencken as 'two streams' of English. American English diverged from the English variety as a result of new circumstances, for example, the need to describe unfamiliar landscapes and weather[128] and as a result of the contacts among people speaking different languages: French, Dutch, German, Spanish, African-Americans, and Native Americans.[129] Not only did the mixing of peoples produce new words, but also the circumstances of the encounters produced new contexts for old words, changing their meanings.[130] American English had diverged so markedly by 1812 that 'almost every English traveler of the years between the War of 1812 and the Civil War was puzzled by the strange signs on American shops'.[131]

Most significantly for purposes of confronting Roosevelt's story of the 'winning of the west' by the 'English-speaking peoples', despite attempts to standardize American English in order to build a unique national culture (Noah Webster's primary motivation)[132] what resulted was a hybrid tongue, a product of cultural encounters, with Native American language speakers among others. As Mencken noted, 'the earliest Americanisms were probably borrowed bodily from Indian languages',[133] and it remains the case that many place names, animal and food names, as well as action and situation words come from Native American languages.

Rather than having been merely driven off, Native Americans left lasting cultural markers on 'America'. Apart from contributions to American English, Native American agricultural practices, alliance strategies, military technologies and methods, and other cultural practices helped to create what are now both European and American institutions and practices.[134] Certainly, many of the Native American cultures became to some extent Europeanized, but it is also the case that English colonial culture became, in part, Indianized, with lasting historical effects.[135]

Just as Canaanites and Arabs shared in the production of 'Israel,' – historically, they were neither an absence nor a mere obstacle – Native Americans have had a significant co-operative role in constituting the 'America' that was shaped as it was extended westwards. A genealogical as opposed to legendary account of the constitution of the Native American other by Euro-Americans reveals an initial period of in some ways respectful 'foreign relations' (despite European conceits about cultural superiority). For roughly a hundred and fifty years before 'American independence', colonists negotiated agreements with Native Americans as if they were other nations worthy of recognition, and the various Native American nations (nations which were dispersed into autonomous rather than centralized tribal collectives) were important players in the struggles among different European colonials.[136]

Native Americans were re-situated as domestic hindrances during the Jacksonian period, when Congress and the President, supporting Euro-American demands for territory, chose to ignore the earlier treaties and subsequent legal decisions that had granted tribes a degree of nationhood with respect to their territorial practices.[137] And various forms of American 'knowing' accompanied the political impetus for the changing construction of the Native American. American anthropology, for example, was deeply implicated in the process through which Native American peoples had their identities reordered as they were changed from 'nations' into 'races', where in the context of the former, Euro- and Native American relations were 'foreign policy' and in the context of the latter, 'domestic policy'. After a period of ambiguity in which 'American governments and ethnographers vacillated ambivalently in their conceptualization of Indian Otherness,'[138] both were ultimately complicit in wholly domesticating 'Indians' within sociological and cultural frames that effaced the national frontiers of the North American continent.

Roosevelt's spatial history to the contrary notwithstanding, the winning of the west involved, among other things, the changing of a legal frontier into a domesticated region with an accompanying alteration of the western ethnoscape. Moreover, while Roosevelt represented the movement west of the 'English-speaking peoples' as a series of violent conquests, in which 'The Indians have shrunk back before the advance only after fierce and dogged resistance,'[139] ethno-historical inquiry reveals instead a cultural encounter at a frontier that served as a 'school'[140] in which Native Americans assisted Euro-Americans in their adaptation to an unfamiliar landscape. The spatial encounter was co-operative as well as violent and in many ways co-productive: 'Indians and Old World invaders met, traded, and fought, sometimes with each other, sometimes with themselves. As they struggled to control a particular corner of the continent, they created new landscapes, new property systems, new social relationships, and new political institutions.'[141]

The Euro-Native American co-operation was more extensive than what was ultimately produced as various ways of living *in* the west. Despite the popular assumption that the West was 'won' by over-coming Indian resistance, in various ways, Native Americans assisted in the Euro-American westward advance. The myth of the self-reliant, pioneer/Indian fighter, which has been a significant part of the legendary American nation-building story, is belied by historical investigations into the effects of the 'Covenant Chain', a treaty between Iroquois nations and the Euro-American colonists. The confederation between the Iroquois and the colonists not only helped the English colonists defeat the French (as well as helping to keep the peace between colonists and Native Americans in the eastern zones) but also helped to open the western regions for English settlement.[142]

Francis Jennings' collaborative story of the movement westwards dispels a series of mythic construction of American nation-building: the one that arrogates all significant achievements to the 'white race', the one that constructs American institutions as culturally homoge-nous, and most essentially, the Rooseveltian myth of the 'Indians' as barriers to westward expansion.[143]

Interventions

It remains unclear if the age of nationalism is near an end, but one of its primary legacies remains well entrenched. The story of a unified national culture, designed to legitimate the ethnic and spatial boundary policing of the modern state, continues to play a role in practices of inclusion and exclusion. Contemporary 'strangers in the land' are constructed as threats to legendary and anachronistic national imaginaries. The accounts I have offered – of the highly contingent and often arbitrary commingling of peoples and the resulting co-inventions responsible for what have been historically rendered as autonomous cultural achievements – are meant as interventions. The aim, at the level of writing, has been to disrupt such national imaginaries by contextualizing them in juxtaposition to other scenes, while, at the same time, offering an alternative language and thus an alternative vision.

A primary sustaining mechanism of the American national fantasy is the grammar of its producers. To paraphrase Nietzsche, the only reason people believe in 'America' – as a fixed enduring cultural entity – is because they believe in grammar. Diametrically opposed to the Nietzschean insight that 'America' is in a perpetual state of becoming, an unfinished, and contested terrain of co-invention rather than a fixed entity, is Allen Brimelow's 'will to truth'. Despite all his data displays (in the section of his *Alien Nation* entitled 'Truth'), Brimelow constructs the cultural core of America with his grammar, not with his evidence. He asserts, for example, that 'slowly, over generations, America changed the Irish'.[144] 'America' in this grammatical construction is located as a unified actor/entity. Whereas what constitutes 'America' at any moment are the forces contending to shape it – Irishness, among other cultural practices, contributed to that shaping – Brimelow fabulates an arbitrary cutoff to the shaping process. His American scene opens shortly after Anglo colonists arrive, 'America' has become *a* culture. This fixed unity then acts upon others or is, in turn, threatened by an alien presence impervious to its ability to assimilate it. His 'truth', in short, is a lie, but the lie is lent a variety of rhetorical extensions. He likens his fabricated American culture, for example, to a delicate ecology liable to destruction by various imported new species: 'Thus, the culture of a country, exactly like its ecology, turns out to be a living thing, sensitive and even fragile.'[145]

The appropriate intervention in the grammatical production of such nativist 'truths' is genealogical. The polemical thrust of my analysis operates through the historical juxtapositions I have assembled. The ethno-histories of Israel and America, for example, should be understood as part of an intervention conducted through a historical montage. The jumps and cuts into different times and scenes disrupt 'metahistorical deployments of ideal significations'[146] such as 'America' or 'Israel'. As Foucault has noted, genealogy opposes attempts to 'fabricate[s] a coherent identity'[147] and reduce[d] 'diversity'.[148]

Even more significant than the grammatical construction of such entities as 'America,' and 'Israel' has been the primary discursive mechanism of their historical realization, the legendary stories through which they have been rendered as unitary national cultures. Again, ethno-histories should serve to compromise the mythical accounts. However, if culturally dangerous strangers are to be seen as part of an ongoing history of encounter and co-invention, it is necessary not only to compromise legendary stories but also to tell different ones. Hence, Ammiel Alcalay's story, which recovers Levantine culture, is one that can allow 'Israel' to be constructed as a place of co-invention and the 'Jew' and 'Arab' as culturally imbricated historical characters.[149] And the frontier story of Cronon, Miles, and Gitlin displaces a legend of heroic and autonomous conquest and nation-building by white Euro-Americans with one that registers the cultural sharing and co-operative institution-building that paralleled the more contentious and violent aspects of Euro- and Native American encounters.[150]

Employing the idea of a 'frontier', not to deny the existence of those who live beyond it but to open the problem of identity to ambiguity and adjustment, to a space of becoming rather than territorialization and fortification, provides a different 'American' scene. Such a scene comes into focus through a time image that, in the case of the current American anti-immigrant hysteria, shows how the fetishization of national space is implicated in rendering the stranger as a threat.[151]

Exclusionary modes of nationalism, like racism, are theories as well as practices; as Balibar has noted, racism requires theory.[152] But theory-driven nationalism and national fantasy structures can be disrupted with theoretical (and therefore practical) interventions. The theoretical/practical interventions in this chapter provide alternative stories that denaturalize national space by recounting the 'spatial events' (cultural encounters that reshape the relationship of place to identity)[153] through which structures of habitation have been invented and modes of selfhood have already incorporated various forms of otherness. However, there are also more specific modes of enactment in various artistic genres that serve to attenuate strangeness and overcome the distance that legendary, nation-building stories have encouraged. For example, both Israeli and American cinema have provided important interventions in the dominant national stories that construct the culturally dangerous alien-other.

In the Israeli case, the history of cinema is a history of a gradual shift from an immediate post-independence realist genre that was heroic-nationalistic (such as celebratory accounts of the independence war against Arabs) to more avant garde, in some cases surrealist, genres that challenge the warfare and security bases of the Israeli state, for example, the heroic historical story of Israeli nation-building, and the hegemony of the Euro-oriented, Ashkenazi Israeli.[154]

Unlike the official discourse, contemporary Israeli cinema has attacked the Israeli nationalist story of a unified culture. Without treating the range of films that have attempted to 'shatter the perception of a collective Israeli identity',[155] Rafi Bukai's *Avanti-Populi* (1986) is especially worth mentioning. Unlike the more nationalistic films, it makes use of Israeli Palestinians as actors (playing the role of Egyptians during the 1967 Six Day War), and it sidesteps the Israeli–Arab dichotomy, foregrounding instead those with peace-seeking versus war-mongering positions. It dissolves the estrangement between Israeli and Egyptian soldiers, particularly in a moment when an Egyptian soldier adopts a Jewish persona and recites a Shylock speech from *The Merchant of Venice*.[156]

American cinema, which has alternatively promoted and challenged the dominant national fantasy, is of course too vast to summarize, but, John Sayles's film *Lone Star* (1996) is pertinent here because it constitutes a dramatic intervention into the framing of policy discourse related to 'illegal aliens' from Mexico. The story takes place in a Texas town that has a Mexican–American majority but is dominated by Anglo officials. The heroic legends surrounding the battle of the Alamo hang heavily over the town, estranging Euro- and Mexican Americans. A verbal war over the history of the region takes place in a scene at a school board meeting where Anglo board members complain about the alternative, Mexican points of view being provided by teachers at the local high school. The problem of contested national and state legends that divide people is paralleled by the problem of a local legend. The Anglo-dominant city council plans to honour a deceased, legendary sheriff, Buddy Deeds, by naming a park after him, over the protests of the more politicized segment of the town's Mexican–American community. The legend's son, Sam, is now the (ambivalent) sheriff. When a body is discovered, that of the former sheriff (with whom Sam's father had exchanged treats) who had been missing for over thirty years, it is Sam's responsibility to solve the crime. Sam's investigation, which uncovers a complicated set of local biographies, suggests that Buddy Deeds may have committed a murder.

Less important than the murder investigation are the discoveries that disclose personal connections among various ethnically and nationally diverse persons in the drama, as the problem of fixing personal (hi)stories runs parallel with the ambiguity of the aggregate history of the Alamo. The political impetus of the film is captured in two conversations that foreground the ambiguities of territorial division, identity, and history.

First, Sam's investigation reveals the complex Mexican–American cultural transactions that national boundaries cannot inhibit. The fragility of the Mexican–US border, across which many of the relevant characters in his story have travelled, is emphasized by a used tyre merchant in Mexico, a former 'illegal alien' who had lived for a while on the American side of the border. The man asks Sam to cross a line he draws in the sand on his lot (not incidently using a Coca Cola bottle – a global product that ignores boundaries – to draw the line) and then tells him how much less power his interrogation has on one side versus the other.

Second, the story of the production of the town's ethnoscape, which produces various personal ambiguities, is treated in a conversation between O, a black bar owner and unofficial major of the black community, and his grandson. O is caught up in complicated personal story because his estranged son, now an army colonel in charge of the local army base, is back in town. O finally meets his grandson, to whom he tells the story about how the family contains 'mixed blood' (some of their ancestors are Seminoles). But, O notes, in a remark central to what the film conveys, 'blood only means what you let it'.

O's remark takes on an additional resonance when Sam, who has become romantically involved with his former high school sweetheart, Pilar, learns that they are brother and sister (Pilar is a product of Buddy Deed's extra-marital affair with Mercedes, her mother). Like O, Sam and Pilar don't let it mean too much; they remain romantically involved despite their 'blood' relationship. Sayles does not want it to mean too much either. And he wants us to forget certain (hi)stories, like that of the Alamo and other stories that allow the border between Mexico and America, and between Anglos, Mexicans, and blacks to mean too much: 'sometimes you just have to forget history', he says.[157]

Lone Star's disruption of the historical tradition of ethnic and political boundary-drawing, which characterizes much of the border area of the US south-west, operates within its camera consciousness as well as its verbalized thematics. Through various flashbacks and juxtapositions, the sequence of shots creates a pluralistic and contentious past instead of the absolute, immutable past that would have been conveyed by a camera that simply followed action in a chronological sequence.

Within a Kantian model of recollection, the present emerges from the past for everyone in the same way, because temporality is intrinsic to a universalistic mental faculty. But the condition of possibility for *Lone Star*'s contentious past is a cinematic faculty. Gilles Deleuze, referring to the relationship between brain and world, notes that cinematic memory is specifically not a matter of showing a mental faculty as it engages in recollection. Rather, in cinematic thought, the memory effect '*makes* sheets of past and layers of reality correspond',[158] thereby indicating how various relationships co-exist. The cinematic faculty is thus not comparable to a psychological memory but is rather what Deleuze calls a 'strange faculty' that connects the domain of the individual with that of the collective, or, as he puts it, 'private business' with 'the people's business'.[159]

The cinematic author/director of modern political cinema (exemplified in Sayles's *Lone Star*), as Deleuze has constructed her or him, is homologous with the author problematic of this chapter. What must be directed is the undoing of stories:

> The cinema author finds himself before a people, which, from the point of view of culture, is doubly colonized: colonized by stories that have come from elsewhere, but also by their own myths become impersonal entities at the service of the colonizer.[160]

Moreover and significantly, Sayles heeds Deleuze's injunction that the cinematic author 'must not make himself an ethnologist of his people', must not 'invent a fiction which would be one more private story'.[161] Sayles's commitment to forgetting history is an important part of his resistance to essentializing any story that would allow unambiguous identity claims.

Conclusion: Immigrant Counter-imaginaries

Sayles is not alone in his artistic/political enactments, and progressive cinema is but one kind of intervention into border policing mentalities.

In another venue of the Mexican–US border a group of artists who call themselves ADOBE LA ('Architects, Artists and Designers Opening the Border Edge of Los Angeles') have produced installations, performances, and documentaries about immigrant life that intervene in the imaginative construction of the immigrant.[162] They refer to themselves as 'coyotes with sketch books and video cameras' who advocate 'the "Tijuanization of LA".'[163]

Finally, I want to conclude with an account of another public artist's more general intervention in the construction of the immigrant, because it recalls the more immediate visual reaction to immigrants of that early twentieth-century 'scholar'/Jeremiah, E. A. Ross, a character who appeared in the opening scene of this historical montage. Recognizing that how the immigrant is seen in public space results from the imposition of alienating imaginaries rather than the immigrants' own accounts of themselves, Krzysztof Wodiczko has produced a radical extension of the immigrant body. He supplies selected immigrants with hi-tech prostheses that are obtrusive enough to interrupt the ascriptions that the immigrants' unaided presence would produce. They are so eye-catching that they draw people close enough to provoke encounters between the immigrants and local residents. In effect, they help the immigrant to intervene in the process by which a contemporary Ross might typecast them within their national and global imaginaries.

One of Wodiczko's inventions is a *bâton d'étranger* (alien staff). Resembling the rod of a biblical shepherd, it is equipped with a mini-video, running a short biographical sketch of the wearer, and a loudspeaker, powered by batteries the wearer carries in a shoulder bag. The small image on the screen induces observers to move closer for a better look, diminishing 'the usual distance between the operator, the stranger and the passers by'.[164] The staff gives the stranger a 'double presence' – one in life and one in media – that stimulates reflection on how persons are constructed in imagination versus how they exist within their personal life-worlds. Wodiczko intends this alteration of the mode of presencing immigrants to allow them to become more legitimate and real; the aim, he notes, is to provoke 'an incitement to infringe on the barrier between stranger and non-stranger'.[165]

Another identity-disrupting piece of equipment Wodiczko has created for immigrants to wear is a *porte-parole* (mouthpiece) that covers the wearer's mouth like a gag. It also has a small video monitor and speakers, creating a 'speechless stranger' whom Wodiczko conceives as 'a teller of prophetic stories . . . a poetic interrupter of established life in public space and dominant culture'.[166] The intent is to portray the absurdity of imposing meanings on strangers while depriving them of a voice at the same time. The device restores a means of saying; it is an enactment that comports well with Emmanuel Levinas's ethical commitment to an absolute respect in encounters with alterity and his corollary that this respect can be achieved only if the 'said', the preconceived frames within which the other is understood, is displaced by a 'saying', a speech act that disrupts the incorporation of the other's past into a thematized, already 'said'.[167]

Significantly for purposes here, Wodiczko's political and necessarily public art makes use of Jeremiah's genre – the pronouncement in public space – to oppose the traditional Jeremiad. Instead of warning of the corrupting affects of the strangers in our midst, of the perils of cultural assimilation, he provokes encounter rather than counselling estrangement. And, importantly, his art is not deployed to counter mere individual bigotry. What he calls *art étranger* 'crosses the individual–collective frontier'.[168] It seeks to interrupt not only the dynamic of communication between individual stranger and inhabitant/observer but also the circulated modes of the discourse of the state propagated to consolidate its power.[169] The state's consolidating discourse on national culture, which imposes an alienating script on the stranger, becomes, in Wodiczko's conceits, a package of 'dangerous metaphors'. His artistic enactments are meant to 'disarm or deactivate' them.[170] The analysis here is meant to serve the same purpose. Culture is a dynamic that moves on, despite, not because of, state cultural productions and national master narratives; it emerges from encounters and negotiations. Unified and fixed national cultures are inventions, fantasies designed to legitimate the idea of a 'nation-state'. Once one relaxes territorial models of identity and recognizes the amoeba-like historical presencing of cultural boundaries,[171] there can be no culturally dangerous others, only dangerous ways of fixing 'culture'.

Notes

1. Immanuel Kant, 'Perpetual Peace', trans. H. B. Nisbet, in Hans Reiss (ed.), *Political Writings* (New York: Cambridge University Press).
2. Immanuel Kant, *Anthropology from Pragmatic Point of View*, trans. Victor Lyle Dowdell (Carbondale: Southern Illinois University Press, 1978), p. 251.

3. Jeffrey Rosen, 'The War on Immigrants', *The New Republic*, 212 (30 January 1995), pp. 22–6.

4. Eric Schmitt, 'English as Official Language Wins Backing of House Panel', *New York Times* 25 July 1996, p. A 11.

5. John Higham, *Strangers in the Land* (New Brunswick, NJ: Rutgers University Press, 1955).

6. John C. Miller, *Crisis in Freedom: The Alien and Sedition Acts* (Boston: Little Brown, 1951), p. 41.

7. Edward Alsworth Ross, *The Old World in the New* (New York: The Century Co., 1914), p. 299.

8. Balibar notes that 'meta-racists' displace the race concept onto a cultural one. They rely, he argues, on a theory of anthropological culturalism. See Étienne Balibar, 'Is there a "Neo-Racism"?' in Étienne Balibar and Immanuel Wallerstein, *Race, Nation, Class*, trans. Chris Turner (New York: Verso, 1991), pp. 18–34. Employing Balibar's meta-racism concept, Renata Salecl does a compelling analysis of national discourses surrounding the violence in the former Yugoslavia: Renata Salecl, 'The Fantasy Structure of Nationalist Discourse', *Praxis International*, 13:3 (October 1993), pp. 213–23.

9. Lawrence Auster, *The Path to National Suicide: An Essay on Immigration and Multiculturalism* (Monterey, Virginia: The American Immigration Control Foundation, 1990).

10. Cultural suicide is the most general danger to which Allen Brimelow's book seems to refer. See Allen Brimelow, *Alien Nation* (New York: Random House, 1995).

11. Ross, *The Old World in the New*, p. 286.

12. Ibid., p. 288.

13. Jonathan Crary, *Techniques of the Observer* (Cambridge, Mass.: MIT Press, 1991), p. 9.

14. Ibid., p. 20.

15. Ibid., p. 48.

16. See Higham, *Strangers in the Land*, p. 134.

17. In addition to Auster's *The Path to National Suicide* and Brimelow's *Alien Nation*, Richard Brookhiser's *The Way of the WASP: How it Made America, and How it Can Save it, So to Speak* (New York: Free Press, 1991) is exemplary of this genre.

18. This concern with a 'population' is an exemplary aspect of the politics of modernity. As Michel Foucault has pointed out, by the eighteenth century, forces such as demographic expansion, monetary abundance, and agricultural growth encouraged

governments to turn to the problem of managing an economy and to 'security', the policing of the boundaries within which this management of people in relation to things was to take place. States became preoccupied with the 'population . . . as the ultimate end of government': Michel Foucault, 'Governmentality', in Graham Burchell, Colin Gordon, and Peter Miller (eds), *The Foucault Effect* (Chicago: University of Chicago Press, 1991), p. 100.

19. Brimelow, *Alien Nation*, p. 179.
20. Ibid., p. 28.
21. Ross, *The Old World in the New*, p. 287.
22. Brimelow, *Alien Nation*, p. 47.
23. Ibid., p. 63.
24. Étienne Balibar, 'Racism and Nationalism', in Balibar and Wallerstein, *Race, Nation, Class*, p. 43.
25. Ross, *The Old World in the New*, p. 95.
26. Brimelow, *Alien Nation*, p. 159.
27. Ibid., p. 33.
28. Ibid., p. 5.
29. Horace M. Kallen, 'Democracy Versus the Melting-Pot: A Study of American Nationality', Part I, *The Nation*, 100, 18 February 1915, p. 193.
30. Ibid.
31. Wade Graham, 'Masters of the Game', *Harpers* (July 1996), p. 36.
32. Ibid.
33. Ibid.
34. Ibid.
35. This story is well told in Jacques Donzelot, *The Policing of Families*, trans. Robert Hurley (New York: Pantheon, 1979).
36. Roxanne Doty, 'The Double-Writing of Statecraft: Exploring State Responses to Illegal Immigration', *Alternatives* 21 (1996), p. 14. Doty's analysis here is based on Homi Bhabha's discussion of the disjunctions inherent in a state's narration of it coherence: 'DissemiNation: Time, Narrative, and the Margins of the Modern Nation', in Homi Bhabha (ed.), *Nation and Narration* (New York: Routledge, 1990)
37. Ibid.
38. Ibid.
39. Ibid.
40. Ibid., p. 16.

41. Ibid.
42. Bhabha, *Nation and Narration*.
43. Jonathan Boyarin, 'Space, Time, and the Politics of memory', in Jonathan Boyarin (ed.), *Remapping Memory: The Politics of TimeSpace* (Minneapolis: University of Minnesota Press, 1994), p. 15.
44. Brimelow, *Alien Nation*, p. 222.
45. Balibar, 'Racism and Nationalism', p. 49.
46. Cindy Patton, 'Tremble, Hetero Swine!', in Michael Warner (ed.), *Fear of a Queer Planet* (Minneapolis: University of Minnesota Press, 1993), p. 163.
47. Michel Foucault, 'The Order of Discourse', trans. Ian McLeod, in Michael J. Shapiro (ed.) *Language and Politics* (New York: NYU Press, 1984), p. 116.
48. For a similar argument, see Kate Manzo's discussion of 'nationalism as scripture' in her *Creating Boundaries: The Politics of Race and Nation* (Boulder, CO: Lynne Rienner, 1996), pp. 37–70.
49. Edmund Leach, 'The Legitimacy of Solomon', in Michael Lane (ed.), *Structuralism: A Reader* (London: Jonathan Cape, 1970), pp. 248–92.
50. Ibid., p. 257.
51. Ibid., p. 258.
52. Ibid., p. 266.
53. Ibid., pp. 271–4.
54. Johannes Pedersen, *Israel: Its Life and Culture*, vol I (London: Oxford University Press, 1926), p. 12.
55. I am using the concept of ethno-history to refer simply to 'the use of ethnological methods and materials' to investigate historical-cultural encounters. But, in addition, I am juxtaposing ethno-history, which treats the changes in cultures and the process of acculturation, to mythological histories that impose fixed cultural identities rather than registering the ambiguous boundaries between various peoples as they co-invent cultural forms and practices. See James Axtell, *The European and the Indian* (New York: Oxford University Press, 1981), p. 5.
56. Pederson, *Israel: Its Life and Culture*, vol I, p. 21.
57. For a general description of the relationships see Christiana van Houten, *The Alien in Israelite Law* (Sheffield JSOT Press, 1991).
58. Ibid., p. 67.
59. Pederson, *Israel: Its Life and Culture*, vol. I, p. 26.

60. The explicative literature on deconstruction is vast. Perhaps the Ur-text with the most thorough rehearsal of the critical dimensions, with a strong application, is Jacques Derrida's *Of Grammatology*, trans. Gayatri Spivak (Baltimore: Johns Hopkins University Press, 1976).

61. Pederson, *Israel: Its Life and Culture* Vol I., p. 35.

62. Ibid., p. 28.

63. Johannes Pederson, *Israel: Its Life and Culture*, vol. IV (London: Oxford University Press, 1940), p. 466.

64. Ibid., p. 471.

65. Max Weber, *Ancient Judaism*, trans. Hans Gerth (New York: The Free Press, 1952), p. 268.

66. Ibid., p. 278.

67. Ibid., p. 285.

68. Houten, *The Alien in Israelite Law*, p. 60.

69. Ibid., p. 53.

70. For a general analysis of this intolerance of multiethnicity, see Pierre L. Van Den Berghe, 'The Modern State: Nation-Builder or Nation-Killer', *International Journal of Group Tensions*, 22:3 (Fall 1992), pp. 191–208.

71. Avner Ben-Amos, 'An Impossible Pluralism? European Jews and Oriental Jews in the Israeli History Curriculum', *History of European Ideas*, 18:1 (1994), p. 41.

72. Daphna Golan, 'Between Universalism and Particularism: The "Border" in Israeli Discourse,' *South Atlantic Quarterly*, 94:4 (Fall 1995), p. 1058.

73. Ibid., p. 1059.

74. Seth Schwartz, 'Language, Power and Identity in Ancient Palestine', *Past and Present*, no. 148 (August 1995), p. 19.

75. Ibid., p. 4.

76. Ibid., p. 45.

77. James Barr, *Comparative Philology and the Text of the Old Testament* (Winona Lake, Indiana: Eisenbrauns, 1987), p. 36.

78. Ibid., p. 15.

79. Nurith Gertz, 'A World without Boundaries: Israeli National Identity in the Eighties as Expressed in Cinema and Literature', *Discours Social/Social Discourse*, 4:3 (summer 1992), p. 156.

80. Ibid.

81. See Gertz 'A Word without Boundaries' for examples.

82. See Ammiel Alcalay, *After Jews and Arabs: Remaking Levantine Culture* (Minneapolis: University of Minnesota Press, 1993).

83. Tamar Katriel, and Aliza Shenhar, 'Tower and Stockade: Dialogic Narration in Israeli Settlement Ethos,' *The Quarterly Journal of Speech*, 76:4 (November 1990), pp. 359–80.
84. Ibid., p. 361.
85. Ben-Amos, 'An Impossible Pluralism?'.
86. Golan, 'Between Universalism and Particularism', p. 1061.
87. See Stephen Franklin, 'Imported workers bringing foreign problems to Israel', *Chicago Tribune* (14 July 1996), Section 1, p. 3.
88. See the monograph issue of *History and Memory*, (7:1 (spring/summer 1995), which treats the contemporary politics of Israeli historiography, focusing on Zionist histories versus its competitors.
89. Myra Jehlen, *American Incarnation* (Cambridge, MA: Harvard University Press, 1986).
90. The expression 'violence of representation' occurs in Jacques Derrida's critical reading of the thought of Emmanuel Levinas: 'Violence and Metaphysics', in *Writing and Difference*, trans. Alan Bass (Chicago: University of Chicago Press, 1978), pp. 79–153.
91. Edward Said, 'Michael Walzer's "Exodus and Revolution" ': A Canaanite reading', *Grand Street*, 5 (1986), pp. 86–106.
92. Ibid., pp. 104–5.
93. Ibid., p. 3.
94. Ibid., p.4.
95. Sacvan Bercovitch, *The American Jeremiad* (Madison: University of Wisconsin Press, 1978), p. 4.
96. Ibid.
97. Ibid., p. 15.
98. Ibid.
99. Ibid., p. 38.
100. Ibid., p. 93.
101. Richard Slotkin, *Regeneration Through Violence: The Mythology of the American Frontier, 1600–1860* (Middletown, Connecticut: Wesleyan University Press, 1973), p. 4.
102. Ibid., p. 22.
103. Ibid., p. 46.
104. Ibid., p. 47.
105. Mark Selzer, *Bodies and Machines* (New York: Routledge, 1992), p. 149.
106. Ibid.
107. Brimelow, *Alien Nation*, p. 210.

108. Ibid.
109. E. A. Ross does not mention Roosevelt, but for him also, those Euro-Americans to whom he credits the 'winning of the west' are the significant actors involved in constituting America. Drawing on the then still influential social Darwinism afflicting American social science, Ross argued that the movement westward: helped to sort out a stronger American 'stock'

> No doubt the 'run of the continent' has improved the fiber of the American people. Of course the well established and the intellectuals had no motive to seek the West; but in energy and venturesomeness those who sought the frontier were superior to the average of those in their class who stayed behind. It was the pike rather than the carp that found their way out of the pool. (*The Old World in the New*, p. 23)

110. Ibid., p. 285.
111. Ibid., p. 290.
112. Theodore Roosevelt, *The Winning of the West* (New York: G. P. Putnam's Sons, 1889), p. 17.
113. Ibid., p. 119.
114. Ibid., p. 30.
115. Ibid.
116. Ibid., p. 40.
117. Ibid., p. 119.
118. Ibid.
119. Frances Fitzgerald, *America Revised* (Boston: Atlantic Monthly, 1979), p. 77.
120. Ibid., p. 78.
121. Ibid., p. 90.
122. Ibid., p. 91.
123. Ibid.
124. Albert C. Baugh and Thomas Cable, *A History of the English Language*, 4th edn, (London: Routledge, 1951), p. 72.
125. Ibid., p. 93.
126. Ibid.
127. H. L. Mencken, *The American Language* (New York: Alfred A. Knopf, 1943).
128. Ibid., p. 3.
129. Ibid., p. 108.
130. Ibid., p. 121.
131. Ibid., p. 12.
132. Webster's role is noted in both Mencken's *The American*

Language, p. 9, and in Baugh and Cable's *A History of the English Language*, pp. 360–2.

133. Mencken, *The American Language*, p. 104.
134. See for example, Jack Weatherford, *Indian Givers* (New York: Fawcett/Columbine, 1988).
135. James Axtell, *The European and the Indian* (New York: Oxford University Press, 1981), p. 273.
136. Marie-Jeanne Rossignol, 'Early Isolationism Revisted: Neutrality and Beyond in the 1790s,' *Journal of American Studies*, 29:2 (August 1995), p. 219.
137. Wilcombe E. Washburn (ed.), *The Indian and the White Man* (New York: New York University Press, 1964). p. 119.
138. John Borneman, 'American Anthropology as Foreign Policy', *American Anthropologist*, 97 (1995), p. 667.
139. Roosevelt, *The Winning of the West*, p. 39.
140. Axtell, *The European and the Indian*, p. 133.
141. William Cronon, George Miles, and Jay Gitlin, 'Becoming West,' in Cronon et al. (eds), *Under and Open Sky: Rethinking America's Western Past* New York: W. W. Norton, 1992), p. 7.
142. Francis Jennings, *The Ambiguous Iroquois Empire* (New York: W. W. Norton, 1984), p. xvii. As Jennings elaborates, the five-nation Iroquois participation in the Covenant Chain involved a division of labour. For example, Mohawks were keepers of the easter door and Senecas keepers of the western door. Ultimately, Iroquois diplomacy, rather than their mere military co-operation in the war with the French, set the stage for English westward migration. As Jennings puts it, 'English sovereignty claims westward depended primarily on Iroquois accomplishments'(Ibid., p. 173). Attention to the co-operative aspects of the story of settlement, in which Iroquois and other Native American peoples helped to facilitate movement westwards and shape American practices, violates mainstream political and anthropological theory. From the point of view of political theory and consequently 'American' political history, the Covenant Chain is not recognized as part of the United States' nation-building story because 'there is no existing theory or ideology that has room for it' (Ibid., p. 38). What takes up all the room, he notes, is the traditional sovereignty discourse which requires an unambiguous cultural centre. The co-operative story violates anthropological theory because 'it does not fit an evolutionary scheme of any kind because it was unique', (Jennings, and it does not fit a

functional approach either when applied to given cultures because it was 'bi-societal and bi-cultural'(Ibid., p. 39)).

143. As Jennings summarizes it:

> Despite the fascination of European observers and writers with the otherness of Indians, it was human similarity that created great institutions of commerce and politics through which Indians guided Europeans to the interior and collaborated in their exploitation of its vast resources (Ibid., pp. 367–8).

144. Brimelow, *Alien Nation,* p. 215.
145. Ibid., p. 181.
146. Michel Foucault, 'Nietzsche, Genealogy, History', trans. Donald F. Bouchard and Sherry Simon, in Paul Rabinow (ed.), *The Foucault Reader* (New York: Pantheon, 1984), p. 77.
147. Ibid., p. 81.
148. Ibid., p. 86.
149. Alcalay, *After Jews and Arabs.*
150. Cronon, Miles, and Gitlin, 'Becoming West'. Cronon et al.'s story substitutes a spatial for a legendary history. Instead of emphasizing the acts of appropriation accompanying colonization they register the complicated dynamic by which significances have been attributed to inhabited places. They employ the spatial model of the frontier to imply that the cultural confrontation involved a negotiation of relationships between the different groups. The relationship was fluid, non-institutionalized, precarious, and uncertain. Certainly there was considerable violence, but there was also a sense that co-existence required a resistance to fixity on both sides of the encounter.
151. Calling such a fetishization the *'territorial* theory of identity', Ulrich Beck argues that when one removes the issue of identity from the spatial assumption in which it is engendered, 'namely the nation-state, it loses its plausibility' (Ulrich Beck, 'How Neighbors Become Jews: The Political Construction of the Stranger in an Age of Reflexive Modernity', *Constellations,* 2:3 (January 1996), p. 393.
152. Étienne Balibar, 'Is there a "Neo-Racism?" ' in Balibar and Wallerstein, *Race, Nation, Class,* pp.18–34.
153. My use of the concept of a 'spatial event', which reflects the interaction between space and history, is influenced by Kristin Ross, who has applied it to the Paris Commune. As she notes, 'an awareness of social space . . . always entails an encounter with history – or better, a choice of histories' (Kristin Ross, *The*

Emergence of Social Space: Rimbaud and the Paris Commune (Minneapolis: University of Minnesota Press, 1988), p. 8).

154. For an excellent review of the history of Israeli cinema and its significance for complicity versus resistance to official stories, see Ella Shohat, *Israeli Cinema: East/West and the Politics of Representation* (Austin: University of Texas Press, 1987).

155. Nurith Gertz, 'A World without Boundaries', p. 161.

156. Ibid., p. 166.

157. John Sayles, ' "I don't want to blow anything by people': Interviewed by Gavin Smith', *Film Comment* (May-June 1996), p. 58. Sayles enacts his sentiment about not letting history mean too much by the way he constructs the historical development of the composition of the town. It turns out to have a surprising ethno-political history that doesn't mean too much in its daily life. As Sayles puts it:

> As *Lone Star* started to evolve, I wanted to have these three communities; we were basically in a part of Mexico that someone had drawn a line underneath and made into America, but the people hadn't changed. The Anglos got to run things, but it was still basically a Mexican town. (Ibid., p. 60)

158. Gilles Deleuze, *Cinema 2,* trans. Hugh Tomlinson and Robert Galeta (London: Athlone, 1989), p. 207.

159. Ibid., p. 221.

160. Ibid., p. 222.

161. Ibid.

162. Mike Davis, 'Learning from Tijuana', *Granta*, 56 (1995), p. 33.

163. Ibid., p. 36.

164. Krzysztof Wodiczko, *Art public, art critique: textes, propos et documents* (Paris: École Nationale Supérior des Beaux-Arts, 1995), p. 212.

165. Ibid.

166. Ibid., p. 237.

167. Emmanuel Levinas, *Otherwise than Being: Or Beyond Essence,* trans. Alphonso Lingus (The Hague: Matinus Nijhoff, 1981), p. 37.

168. Wodiczko, *Art public, art critique*, p. 206. The performance art of Guillermo Gomez-Peña, who refers to himself as a 'migrant performance artist', constitutes another public intervention into the dominant construction of the alien-other. Constructing and acting out cultural hybrids, Gomez-Pena seeks to attenuate both national borders and the prevailing discourses on cultural types.

See his *The New World Border* (San Francisco: City Lights, 1996).

169. Ibid., p. 48.
170. Ibid., p. 208.
171. The 'amoeba' reference has two encouragements. First, Francis Jennings, in a discussion of the vagaries of various national territorial boundaries, remarks, 'Poland's historical boundaries look like the antics of an amoeba in heat. What indeed shall we properly call the variform and culturally complex entity known as the United States of America?'(Jennings, *The Ambiguous Iroquois Empire*, pp. 37–8). And second, Boaventura De Sousa Santos contrasts 'fortress-communities' with 'amoeba-communities'. The former 'are communities that, whether aggressively or defensively, base internal identification on external closure', while in the latter, 'identity is always multiple, unfinished, undergoing a process of reconstruction and re-invention'. See Boaventura De Sousa Santos, *Toward a New Common Sense* (New York: Routledge, 1995), p. 485.

3

The Politics of 'Globalization'

Every culture, our culture ceaselessly draws up maps of the space of knowledge and of the imaginary, maps accessible everywhere, maps ordered according to cycles of cycles. To inhabit our space, to inhabit concrete space, or the space of knowledge, or the space of culture, is to have one's own place, be it personal or collective, defined by these multiple circles. It is to be immersed, to be coiled up in the security of the warm bosom of these cycles of cycles.

Michel Serres[1]

Father of the Bride II – A Sign of the Times

Events and encounters disturb the ontological security of a social order when they disrupt the modalities of its transactions outside its traditionally marked boundaries. Because territorially organized peoples understand themselves on the basis of the autonomy they ascribe to their spatio-temporal limits and constraints (as well as on the basis of the stories of their founding and persistence), alterations of boundaries or new cross-boundary transactions can threaten to attenuate collective identity. Among the reactions to such disruptions are anxiety-driven political interpretations and initiatives aimed at securing identity boundaries.

The Hollywood feature film *Father of the Bride II* (Charles Shyer, 1995)can be read as a domestic allegory of such identity anxieties. Shot primarily on MGM Studio stages, it understood itself as a 'domestic comedy', focusing on the trauma experienced by a father, George Banks (played by actor/comedian Steve Martin), whose narrative voice, during the introductory segment, expresses his anger at having already been displaced as the primary male figure in his daughter's life by her young husband. In addition to his concern with his family's altered libidinal structure, he worries about its spatial dispersion. The young couple is planning an out-of-state move to pursue their careers.

Banks' anxieties are markedly heightened early in the film. He evinces an aging crisis when he learns that he is to become a grandfather. His identity crisis is played for laughs as he reacts to his aging with a series of frantic moves: working out with weights at an exercise club, dyeing his hair, and reinvigorating his romantic life by having sex with his wife on the kitchen floor. The crisis moves towards resolution when, as an implied result of the kitchen coupling, Mrs. Banks (Diane Keaton) also turns out to be pregnant. This happy news helps to restore the stable domesticity that George felt he had been losing.

But *Father of the Bride II* does not confine itself to crises of domesticity. Opening scenes are exhausted by the exploration of domestic space as the camera pans the various features of a well-appointed bourgeois family home: candelabras, family photos on end tables, and abundant pieces of plush furniture. But once the story moves beyond its mapping of the Banks' family life, global space is explored obliquely. Through the introduction of two resident immigrants, the representation of anxieties attendant to changes in the configuration and spatial extension of the family becomes an allegory of national anxieties associated with changes in the ethnic composition of national space. Two of the story's characters serve as stand-ins for exotic global venues.

Specifically, when subjected initially to a crisis of aging, Banks decides to make a bold move and sell the house that has been the family home for eighteen years. The buyer turns out to be a wealthy Arab, Mr Habib. While the writers and producers represented Habib's role as simply a response to the need to 'modernize' the script,[2] the choice of an Arab, portrayed as a wealthy and predatory businessman acquiring the family home, is symptomatic of a more general contemporary anxiety, the construction of the cultural Other as a threat to the domestic space of the nation as a whole. Samuel Huntington, a 'security analyst' (whom I summon for substantial treatment in a later section) is an articulate exemplar of those who think that the United States – as part of an entity called 'the West' – is threatened by the increasing presence of such cultural Others. He warns against welcoming 'multiculturalism':

> Some Americans have promoted multiculturalism at home, some have promoted universalism abroad, and some have done both. Multiculturalism at home threatens the West; universalism abroad threatens the West and the World. Both deny the uniqueness of Western culture.[3]

Habib's role in the domestic allegory of such threats to 'the West' is immediately apparent. His purchase of Banks' home is unconventional; he wants the house immediately: 'We like the house very much. When you can move? . . . We need the house a week from Wendesday or is no deal', he says in heavily accented English. To achieve the rapid displacement of George Banks and his family from their home, Habib peels off a bonus of $15,000 in thousand dollar denominations from a large money roll he takes from his pocket.

When Banks learns soon after that his wife is pregnant, he rethinks the selling of his house. The camera follows an agitated Banks, walking rapidly up his old street. As he nears his former home, he sees a wrecking ball in motion and spots Mr Habib, who is saying 'bye bye house'. As Banks engages Habib in conversation we hear that for Habib, the house is simply an inconvenience on a 'valuable piece of land.' Begging Habib to sell him back the house, Banks screams, 'this is not a piece of land, this is my *home*' and proceeds to tell Habib that he laid the bricks on the walk, painted the screens, and broke the window with a frisbee. 'Don't bulldoze my memories', he pleads. Habib relents but charges him $100,000 more than he had paid for the house the previous day.

There is a remarkable repression in the construction of Habib as an economic predator. Although Banks is shocked at being faced with a $100,000 surcharge to reacquire his home, his ability to meet the demand, along with his other accoutrements of a wealthy lifestyle – his well-appointed home, expensive car, and exercise-club membership – pass without filmic comment. There are no juxtapositions to suggest that Banks' lifestyle is structurally related to the economic condition of others who are less well off. The camera remains fixed on Banks' personal drama and confines the space of interaction to those who occupy his status niche. Insofar as political economy explicitly enters the story, it is condensed in the form of the dangerously unsentimental Mr Habib.

Habib is more than an item of script modernization. At one level, he is a threat to the domestic space of the family; at another, he is a threat to the territorial/cultural space of the nation. He is a dangerous cultural Other who operates with a different commitment with respect to what is exchangeable versus singular or non-exchangeable because of its special cultural and emotional significance. Moreover, the geography of danger that the Habib character reflects is not incidental to the meaning of the encounter. Habib's identity as an Arab or, more generally, a non-Westerner contrasts with another character in the plot, Frank (pronounced with a soft *a*), an Austrian caterer and interior decorator, who handles the Banks' weddings, house remodelling and baby shower parties. Once the news of the senior Banks baby is shared throughout the family, Frank is hired again, this time to reconfigure and decorate a room for their new baby.

Although it is clear that Frank charges a lot for his services to a wealthy clientele, it is also clear that Frank has more than a strictly business relationship with the family. He is drawn into the domestic preparations for the new babies, leading the women in exercises, giving emotional advice to all family members, and, finally, participating in a hectic scene in which the daughter is going into labour and must be driven to the hospital. Frank literally carries a nearly comatose Banks (who had taken sleeping pills) on his back, dumping him in the car, and driving him and the rest of the family to the hospital.

Again, geographic identity is important, for it is also not incidental that Frank, whose intimacy with the family exceeds a strictly exchange relationship, is also a European. He can be comfortably included within the Banks' cultural imaginary. Moreover, because he is effeminate, and possibly gay, his intimacy with the Banks women constitutes no sexual threat. He does not exacerbate the feelings of masculine rivalry which Banks has already evinced in his poorly disguised rancour towards his son-in-law. At two levels, then, Frank is no threat to the Banks' domesticity.

The threat to domesticity by a non-Western immigrant in *Father of the Bride II* is simply one among many places in which security concerns inflect the reading of global reconfigurations. The film can be read as part of what Fredric Jameson has called a 'geopolitical unconscious'; what is represented as a local (in this case a family) concern refers allegorically to an 'unrepresentable totality', an increasingly complex set of relations between local and global dynamics.[4] The dynamics associated with 'globalization' reconfigure spaces at various levels, provoke cross-boundary flows of people, money, images, and ideas, and put pressure on traditional territorial identities, as distinctions between local and global space become increasingly ambiguous. Moreover, the reconfigurations associated with globalization provoke a wide variety of responses; its meanings and temporal uniqueness are various constructed by diverse groupings within the social order. But two alternative kinds of reactions are especially worthy of scrutiny. On the one hand, globalization provides a frame for thinking the present from the points of view of various identity-securing projects and, on the other, it is a provocation for rethinking the ethics and politics of global hospitality. This particular polarity – security versus hospitality – frames the analysis that follows.

The Problem of Kantian Hospitality

At this juncture, it is appropriate to heed the critical attitude of Immanuel Kant, not only because he provides a counterposition to a security-oriented reading of global events but also because his model of critique provides a frame for a political reading of globalization. From a Kantian perspective, one avoids the naive question: what kind of phenomenon is globalization? Kantian critique encourages inquiry into *how* globalization emerges in various 'productive understandings'. A focus on identity-securing projects, for example, yields an appreciation of how alarmed reactions result from the perception that present global dynamics exceed traditional descriptive and conceptual strategies, as analysts in academia, the media, business, and a wide variety of other fields try both to describe what they render as globalization and to maintain the collective coherence of their identities as they rationalize their practices.

Academic international relations theorists, for example, seek to reconfigure 'American security policy', while those with a more narrow territorial focus, for example psychologists, are adjusting their models of personhood. More generally, there is a rush to reconsider conceptual strategies and alter discourses to adjust various professional and commercial practices, ideational expressions, and geo-political strategies to what is seen as an altered world. But if we heed Kant's insight that there are no things in themselves, that phenomena have the significance they are lent by the imposition of productive understandings, our analysis achieves a distance from the perceptions of the various characters who have located themselves in a crisis narrative. Instead of following their leads, the analysis aims at describing and analyzing that productivity critically by introducing temporal juxtapositions and perspectives. Moreover, by heeding Kant's hospitable reaction to globalizing phenomena, which was part of his commitment to critique, the analysis responds ethically as well as critically to the politics of securing identity.

As was noted in Chapter 2, Kant was alert to a kind of globalizing phenomenon two centuries ago, but he was not alarmed at the global flux that increased his world's encounter with difference. Turning his critical perspective towards the issue of global peace, he was sanguine about the expanding publicity of events. He looked forward both to a future of diminishing global violence and to an expanding global hospitality. The 'moral disposition of the human race' would be increased by the enhanced ability for people all over to read 'the signs of the times':

> The peoples of the earth . . . have entered in varying degrees into a universal community, and it has developed to the point where a violation of rights in *one* part of the world is felt *everywhere*.[5]

Kant's reading of the signs of the times, from which he inferred that 'mankind is improving',[6] was not that of a disinterested observer. The critical thinker/philosopher reads signs not only for purposes of prognostication but also to become a part of history. History, for Kant, is not an objective reality to be merely deciphered; it is an open story, still to be written. In taking part in a 'prophetic history' constructed through a reading of events, 'the prophet himself occasions and *produces* the events he predicts';[7] the critical thinker is one whose public use of reason might nudge humankind in a more positive ethical and political direction.

At an explicit level, then, Kant's position vis-à-vis his readers is polemical rather than hermeneutic. Kantian critique requires an aggressive interpretive appropriation of 'nature' and 'history' rather than a passive reading in order to contribute to a public use of reason and thereby help to engender a hospitable common sense. Although my analysis/writing adopts Kant's anti-hermeneutic approach to both phenomena and his readers, at the same time it resists Kant's appeal to mental faculties, functioning within a universalizing narrative that re-inscribes the hermeneutic that his text seeks to evade. Instead of evoking a growth in common sense, my text is aimed at mobilizing signs rather than merely reading them and at provoking critical thought rather than *a* sanguine interpretation of modernity.

Inspired by the signifying practices immanent in cinematic time images, the writing here is meant to mobilize a mode of thinking that recognizes the radical contingency of the subjects and objects constituted in discourses of persons and spaces. 'Publicity' in some forms – for example, contemporary cinema – is mobilizing because of the way it uses the mobility of its images. Although Kant intended to help encourage an ongoing process of public reasoning, his appeal to a fixed chronology of the participation of mental faculties, ending in a felicitous common sense, imposed a hermeneutic closure on the process of thought that he wished to keep open.

The analysis here resists yet another aspect of Kant's perspective. It seeks to overcome the spatio-temporality of his imaginary as well as his slide into a mentality-oriented hermeneutics. Kant confines the very subjects whose thought he seeks to mobilize because the world in which he imagines the possibility of hospitality and peace is predicated on various forms of radical non-peace. Kant's imagined world is mapped on the basis of state boundaries, and the subjects who inhabit that world are state citizens. Within Kant's perspective, the peaceful sensibility that is encouraged cannot acknowledge the non-peace involved in the settling of spaces that established state boundaries and the non-peace associated with the production of identities that are not comfortably included in the identity of stable citizen subjects.

Stable citizenship subjectivity and national space provided the intelligible bases for Kant's hoped-for, expanding global consciousness and tolerance. Indeed, state space receives a double emphasis in Kant's writings. His geo-political model map is articulated within a state-oriented imaginary at both philosophical and practical levels. And the two levels are structurally homologous, for Kant had a deep respect for both political and conceptual boundaries. The practice of strict geographic separations evident in his philosophical geography – for example, his separation of the noumenal and phenomenal worlds – is evident in his practical geography. His map recognizes no nations that are not part of the map of states. Insofar as there is extra-state space in Kant's world, it exists outside of the boundaries created by land masses. Kant's meta-geography bears traces of the fifteenth-century cartographic imaginary within which the world was 'geographically pictured as an island . . . surrounded by the dark, inhuman and unknowable void of the deep waters'.[8]

Despite the strong ideational effects of such figuration in his geographic imaginary, Kant was conceptually prevented from appreciating the polemical dimensions of his cosmologically invested, geopolitical map. As is evident in his lectures on geography, Kant radically separates geography and history: he states that we learn about the world through *either* stories or descriptions; the former is history and the later is geography. Kantian practical space is thus not infused with historical contingency because Kant's meta-geography locates the domain of stories in a knowledge practice that is isolated from territorial description.[9]

Two aspects of Kantian meta-geography constitute unreflective political missions rather than (what he thought of as) disinterested knowledge commitments. First, in separating geography from history, Kant imagines that he is evoking a universal epistemological practice.

But the separation he takes as a universal insight about knowledge is a culturally relative perspective. Philological comparison reveals, for example, that a geographer and a historian are necessarily distinguished 'in a culture in which writing and mapping become different activities'.[10] The term 'map' in European languages refers to 'the material upon which graphic signs are inscribed'.[11] By contrast, Meso-American cultures used terms for maps whose meanings included scribes and books as well as territorial descriptions.

Kant's separation between geographers and historians therefore participates in an imperialism of meaning, a tendency to universalize Euro-culture; it fails to register the kind of global difference represented by alternative epistemic cultures, such as the Meso-American, which combined geography and history. Meso-American maps provide a more politically acute reading of space, for they reflect the intrication of geography and history; they depict historical encounters as well as the boundaries of territorial, political, and administrative control.[12]

Second, apart from his lack of recognition that his separation of geography from history is a local practice rather than a universal knowledge distinction, Kant's meta-geography participates in constructing the privilege of a state-oriented mode of both space and personhood. His approach to conceptual boundaries can be understood within the same island metaphor as his approach to national boundaries. In his First Critique, he refers to 'the territory of pure understanding' as an 'island', which is a 'land of truth . . . surrounded by a wide and stormy ocean, the native home of illusion.'[13] And his introduction to his *Critique of Judgement* is also telling with respect of his boundary fixations, for there he suggests that faculty of judgement integrates an otherwise heterogeneous set of empirical divisions in the natural world. In a critical response to this gloss on judgement, J. F. Lyotard has introduced a useful set of geographic metaphors that effectively renders Kant's philosophical geography compatible with the Kantian practical geography I have outlined. Lyotard suggests that Kant sought to provide a set of transitions between separate islands of discourse (or 'phrases' in Lyotard's idiom), that in effect he sought to consolidate an integrated archipelago of domains of apprehension. At the level of philosophical discourse, then, Kant sought to create a milieu out of separate domains. His approach to judgement integrates the domains of knowledge, morality, and taste, keeping, in Lyotard's terms, an effective 'commerce' between them.[14] And, it should be added, that at a less metaphorical level, Kant regarded an interest in 'commerce' within the frame of his practical geography as a pacifying one. Commerce, he argued, generates a structure of mutual self-interest that resists the disruptions of war.[15] In the domain of commerce, as in the domain of law, Kant was not attentive to the various dimensions of violence other than war, particularly those aspects of violence involved in consolidating conceptually as well as militarily, the geo-political map.

Certainly, one cannot wholly avoid state geography and citizen subjectivity to treat either Kant's world or the present one intelligibly. Stable national citizenship operates within powerful modes of authority and, as a result, remains an important locus of enunciation. But there are others that are increasingly prominent. If, for example, one looks at images and locutions from the points of view of migrants who have crossed borders and function, as a result, with an ambiguous territorial focus, 'publicity' can have multiple readings. In the case of the contemporary effects of globalization, the confounding of the local and the global produces very different readings of the same transmitted images. The current 'compression of time and space and the consequent "shrinking" of the world' can have 'contradictory outcomes'[16], as Avtal Brah has noted in her treatment of diasporic people.

What shape can critique take if it moves beyond Kantian space and the Kantian notion of a universally apprehended global publicity? It should be noted, first, that the Kantian perspective on publicity shows little sensitivity to what Foucault has called 'the governmentalization of modern identities'. For Foucault, a resistance to the 'self-incurred tutelage' that Kant's critiques were designed to challenge must treat critique as 'the art of not being governed quite so much'.[17] The extension of critique in this direction would extend a cosmopolitan tolerance beyond the geo-political model informing Kant's perspective.

Foucauldian critique is aimed at forms of coercion that are more extensive and subtle than the authoritarian acts of unrestrained sovereigns, which occupied most of Kant's critical attention. Speaking, for example, of the 'coercive structure of the signifier', Foucault calls attention to mechanisms of coercion that extend beyond issues of the legitimacy of governmental forms of the exercise of power and takes criticism beyond the Kantian emphasis on public disclosure. Knowledge, as Foucault points out, does not work its power effects simply on the basis of secrecy and illusion; it also extends itself through 'the production of singularities', through the discursive production of models of subjectivity and space.[18]

Second, it is important to note the ways in which Kant's writing failed its critical mission. Despite his explicit approach to discourse, which emphasized publicity versus secrecy, Kant appreciated 'the coercive power of the signifier' implicitly. Kant's critiques are highly polemical; they abound in rhetorical figures, aimed at persuasion as they deflect thinking away from the sacrilization of entrenched forms of authority and towards an appreciation of the aporias of knowledge and experience. His aim was to displace hierarchically dispensed pronouncements with common sense and, correlatively, the power of both state hegemons and Christian clergy with moral citizens.[19]

But discourse was not constitutive for Kant; he thought an author should strive to represent the structures of comprehension in a way that would disclose the interrelations among the world of things and should, above all, seek to achieve clarity of thought. Although he recognized literariness as a necessary complement to reason in philosophical investigation – reasoning is aided by narrative, he argued, and the story of a given inquiry could begin anywhere and avoid a linear path[20] – he regarded language primarily as an aid to making observations. Polemical though his aims were, Kant employed recognizable expressions in recognizable ways. Although, for example, he wanted national borders to be more porous, that is to be managed with a cosmopolitan tolerance instead of being policed with a nationalistic security-mindedness, his thinking/writing reinforced his century's system of subjects and spaces.

If we move up a century, we can find in Franz Kafka's writing a contrast to Kant's rhetorical participation in the scripting of citizen subjectivity and state space both philosophically and practically. Unlike Kant, Kafka altered linguistic expressions in order to impugn a strictly cognitive mode of apprehension. Regarding common sense or generalized consciousness as delusional, Kafka's writing stages the ambiguities and dangers of the commonly accepted, intelligible world rather than contributing to a reinforcement of existing forms of subjectivity.[21] For this reason, Deleuze and Guattari interpret Kafka's anti-representational approach to writing as a way to disrupt the structures of subjectification in which common language participates. Constructing Kafka as a writer of 'minor literature', they note how those who write from a minoritarian perspective within major literatures resist common sense and provide a politicized mode of apprehension by making space for 'pilgrimages' within the dominant language.[22]

Most significantly, Deleuze and Guattari mobilize Kafka's example to oppose philosophy's reinforcement of the discourse of state dominance. Because minor literature has 'a high coefficient of deterritorialization',[23] it provides a different model of hospitality than one can derive from Kant's cosmopolitan tolerance, based on the reigning territorial structures of states. Its potential for critique goes beyond abuses of authority within the system of recognized sovereignties. Hospitality within the practice of deterritorializing critique is not aimed at particular beings, for example, those identified as border crossers; it is aimed at resisting the fixity of the subject.

A Deleuzian assessment of Kafka's minor literature therefore has implications not only for showing the limits of Kantian common sense but also for reconfiguring the notion of cosmopolitan hospitality. When language disrupts the signifying practices within which the meanings of persons and places are constructed, it undermines the prevailing boundaries of both subjects and territories. If Kantian hospitality arises from a critique of the domains for knowing *about* human subjects, a critique of Kantian hospitality must rest on a questioning of the construction of the geographic imaginaries that give us particular kinds of persons and spaces. It must employ conceptuality in a way that allows territoriality and subjectivity to be mobile rather than fixed. What is encouraged is not a hospitality towards *being*, that is, towards particular kinds of subjects, but towards *becoming*, towards the open possibilities for persons to resist being wholly quarantined within institutionalized and authoritative modes of identification.

Thinking/Staging the Problem of Globalization

Although the stasis of Kantian geography and subjectivity is owed in part to the state-centric imaginary, in which his philosophical and substantive geographies participated, the Kantian treatment of temporality as immanent in subjectivity is also implicated because it released him from considering the contingency of the time imagery in his philosophical discourse. Although Kant recognized that the narrative aspects of his writing involved choices, his stories of experience and achieved common sense followed an idealized movement from subjectivity to publicity. He told a more or less chronological story in which the different domains of apprehension, governed by the different faculties, become harmonized and increasingly communicative as they consummate their movement towards a global common sense.

In stark contrast is what Deleuze and Guattari call doing philosophy on the basis of 'stratigraphic time', where what is treated as before versus after is recognized as a strategic superimposition.[24] Within this model of temporality, the philosopher becomes a cinematic director rather than a narrator, and historical actors become 'conceptual personae',[25] selected from various layers in time and constituted to move the action in a way that allows for a critical thinking of the present. Attentive to this model of temporality, the analysis here seeks to render globalization from a critical perspective by directing an effective staging of a variety of actors, especially those who operate outside of the citizen subjects central to the state model of space.

Maps of national territories represent the modern state's persistent ontological project, its attempt to 'create and recreate a vision, or visions, of its own existence', which gives rise to its 'constellation of discourses and practices which construct the state as a locus of collective meaning, allegiance, and knowledge'.[26] To resist such legitimating projects, which often turn histories of violent encounter into stories of legal evolution, we must read recent alternative mappings against this persistent one. For example, as Donald Carter notes, now 'the very conception of "Europe" as a kind of historical and natural whole is challenged by an increasing heterogeneity'.[27]

This increasing heterogeneity becomes evident when one maps dynamic domains of cultural transaction instead of state boundaries and heeds the stories of actors usually neglected when one follows only the actions of those who locate themselves and their ancestry in a historically continuous way within particular states. Our attention will therefore be drawn to the 'micro narratives' of diasporic individuals and groups rather than to macro stories of nation-building.[28] Instead of the master shot, aimed at the state as a whole, the focus will shift among a variety of sub-units. The radical entanglement between space and narration, enabled by this mobile focus, receives more elaborate treatment below. At this juncture, the focus is on those seeking to secure their boundaries and projects in the face of challenges to their institutionalized geographic imaginaries, to their ideationally shared ways of describing global space.

Spectres of Globalization

Two things about the present are relevant to this part of the analysis. There are manifest effects of technological change on global relations and a poverty of description in response to those changes. A reconfigured set of relationships between local and global spaces, in which changing technologies have disrupted prior territorialities, has challenged the traditional ways of mapping exchanges and power configurations and placed intolerable burdens on various levels of description with which various groups have traditionally come to terms with modern space.

The knowledge practices through which the academic psychology constructs its objects provides an exemplary illustration of a reaction to such a descriptive lacuna. Writing on the challenge of globalization for contemporary psychology, one psychologist constructs globalization as a change in the 'functional units of the social order'.[29] Modern psychology, he suggests, has constituted persons as autonomous individuals in order to achieve a model of personhood that fits with the demands of a social order that had become secularist, democratic, and individualistic (according to his liberal version of modernity). But now, he asserts, 'the theory of the person that was suited to the era of individualization is ill-suited to the era of globalization'.[30]

Certainly the comfortable, depoliticizing metaphor of suitability neglects those centrifugal or recalcitrant aspects of subjectivity that resist centralizing social forces and obscures the historical complicity of academic psychology (and its 'theory of the person') with structures of authority and dominance. 'Globalization' becomes a challenging phenomenon for this psychologist in the context of a depoliticizing project that simply constructs the world as a series of functional relationships between social orders and persons. The relevance of (what the writer qualifies as 'Western') personhood as an object of knowledge is exhausted by its fit within a homogenizing notion of *the* social order. Neglecting structurally induced antagonisms within the order, it is a view that renders psychology complicit with the production of subjectivities that are congenial to the contemporary exercise of power.[31]

Academic psychology shares its felt need to adjust its discourse with a wide range of groups and professions seeking to maintain their coherence in the face of a world that no longer yields itself conveniently to their traditional discursive practices. Three projects in particular are worthy of extended scrutiny because, while they are explicitly aimed at re-establishing collective coherence, they demonstrate significantly similar structures of repression at the same time. Accordingly, my analysis alternatively maps and disrupts the attempt to facilitate the conduct of investment on a global scale (reflected in the pronouncements of Certified Public Accountants (CPAs)), the attempt to expand the domain of 'believers' in the face of an altered map of spiritualities (reflected in the recent statements of Christian ecumenicalists), and the attempt to rethink the issue of security (reflected in the discourse of security analysts). But the direction of the analysis resists the historical chronologies these different professions impose. By substituting a series of historical juxtapositions, my analysis here, as in previous chapters, adopts the form of a literary montage, substituting critical time images for the legitimating ones that each profession evokes in securing a space for its identity coherence.

Certified Public Accountants, Christian ecumenicalists and security analysts all tend to regard 'globalization' as a relatively new challenge to the coherence and integrity of their ideational commitments and professional practices. They emphasize a need to adjust their geographic imaginaries, to re-conceive the terrains within which their activities and thinking are registered and, in many cases, to rethink as well the constituencies relevant to their work. Yet, as they turn their focus on the changing worlds around them, they are haunted by what is within.

Why should we regard an explicit recognition of external exigencies as haunted? Gesturing towards Jacques Derrida's concept of 'hauntology', I am suggesting that in the process of coping with what they construe as a new world (dis)order, these various groups must repress anew – or in Derrida's preferred imagery, 'conjure away' – the aspects of inner disorder and disjuncture that their consolidating languages of order deny.[32] From the more banal consolidation of accountancy in the language of 'national accounting standards', through the more argumentative consolidation of US Christianity into a 'community of believers', to the more ideologically controversial predicate of US security discourse: the assumption of a distinctive, homogeneous, and consensual domestic political culture, the outward gaze, predicated on a unitary framing of the collective observer, is haunted by incoherence within.

More specifically for purposes at hand, the spectres central to Derrida's notion of hauntology undermine the stability of various forms of collective 'being', which are always already afflicted by their repressions of the arbitrary events by which they have been produced and consolidated. They struggle to maintain the fiction of their absolute separation from the various aspects of alterity on which the coherence and singularity of their identities are predicated. Collective forms of being are haunted, in short, because in seeking separation from what is foreign or outside, they repress the foreign territories within, while repressing the ambiguities involved in ascribing a stable territoriality to themselves.

The New World of Accountancy

For CPAs in the United States the primary challenge of globalization has been articulated as an issue of the overly parochial language of accounting. Once aspiring only to a coherent national practice, they are now seeking 'an accounting language transcending national borders', as enterprises become increasingly international.[33] A genealogical reading of the historically changing constructions of the spaces of operation and constituencies of accountants reveals significant modifications in their professional geography since the beginning of the century.

In 1905, the inaugural year of the *Journal of Accountancy*, the world of accountants was wholly national. Accountants sought state recognition for the integrity of their profession in the form of federal legal protections. The accounting profession, asserted one practitioner, must 'receive universal recognition at the hands of the state'.[34] Insofar as there was a relevant world outside US borders, it consisted of exotic accountancy venues. For example, this initial, 1905 volume carried a report on the nature of the German corporation, focusing on its organization and powers. Reports on such venues supplied a pedagogy rather than an immediate challenge, for accountants saw their clientele at this juncture as various domestic firms or manufacturing companies.

Yet the accountant's world, wholly domestic though it was, was haunted. What had been conjured away in the quest for professional integrity, some suspected, was social integrity, or, in the term Hegel suggested for it two centuries ago, *Sittlichkeit* (the ethical life).[35] What asserted itself from time to time on the pages of their professional journals was an attempt to reconcile the accountant as servant of a predatory commercial life with the accountant as concerned and civically responsible citizen. In the 1970s, for example, one writer in the *Journal of Accountancy* explicitly evoked the dual identity of accountant and citizen in a call for 'civic responsibility', especially in behalf of 'the disadvantaged'.[36] The writer's sentiments are predicated on the assumption that the actions of his profession are radically separated from the production of disadvantage; the 'disadvantaged' are represented as mere social facts, existing in a domain external to the practices of the accounting profession.

In the quest to recover the ethical life that a practice embedded in the commercial life may neglect (for example, the writer refers to the valuable voluntary accounting services he offers to the 'disadvantaged'), there is a conjuring-away of the more significant ghosts attendant to capitalism in general. Those phantoms are what the liberal capitalism of the industrial world excludes and represses in its stories of civic virtue: those who are not merely 'disadvantaged' in the sense of (for some unfathomable reason) not sharing in the system's prosperity, but are rather necessarily, that is, structurally, excluded from economic well being. The same structures responsible for the increasing use of professional accounting in order to produce advantage are those that are constitutive of modernity's production of comparative disadvantage. To imagine oneself as both an accountant and as a civically responsible citizen, therefore, one must ignore structural contradictions, while, at the same time, engaging in a more general 'epistemological repression',[37] a denial of the profound and pervasive linkages between political economy and 'ethical' forms of sociality. Although we cannot expect CPAs to be Hegelians or genealogists, by framing their expressed concerns within such critical perspectives, we can understand why it is that *now* the altered space of their functioning has lead them to confound moral and economic discourses. Extensions in the domain of commerce are historically associated with anxieties about appropriate modes of agency in relation to the ethical life. In the sixteenth century, for example, new trade patterns that linked Europe and the western hemisphere with Asia had a marked effect on England's 'moral economy'.[38] Whereas within the traditional English moral economy, work was understood as both a gift and a burden tied to God's charity, a new economic discourse emerged in which calculated aggregates displaced individuals as actors, severing action from traditional ways of constructing responsibility,[39] and as exchange imperatives displaced religious crotchets, the distribution of grain was governed more by practices of hoarding to attain a better profit than by an idea of 'service'.[40] As a result, pamphleteers lamented the dissolution of the connection between religion and economic life.

Similar shifts now afflict the accounting profession. By the late 1980s, it became aware that it was implicated in a global economic system. Having consolidated their position with respect to state recognition of their professional privilege, and having moralized the location of the accountant as a nationally responsible agent, accountants construe the challenge of globalization as a challenge to the discursive frames within which accountants enact their services and develop some stability with respect to whom they serve. Their clientele now exists in a globalized environment; they are more often investors than manufacturers, and those investors are 'disadvantaged', according to one writer, 'if they don't have the information to compare one investment with another'.[41] The accounting body is whole; it is fully recognized within a national domain, but the discursive extension of that body is inadequate because, until recently, there have been different 'accountancy bodies'[42] in different states, each regulating their language and practices only nationally.

Certainly, when accountants served primarily firms and manufacturers, they had stable relationships with face-to-face clients. The stability of this world 'conferred', in Georg Simmel's terms (applied to commercial life in a much earlier period), 'an unrivaled objectivity on the practical content of [professional] life'.[43] And this illusion of objectivity, troubled though it was by what was repressed or excluded, was reinforced by a relatively uniform discourse of accounting. The world of accounting was stabilized in a discourse of accounting categories and procedures, shaped not only by the norms of the profession but also by a uniform national tax code.

Now, serving a world of investors whose decisions operate within disjunctive global venues – different countries have difference tax codes, different controls over investment, and different procedures for valuing inventories – the stability once provided to the accounting profession by a fixed territoriality and fixed normativity no longer exists. As a result, they are addressing what is called 'the move to globalization', referring to the 'reality' of the 'internationalization of capital markets'.[44]

The response to this reality is an attempt to standardize, at a global level, the language of accounting, while, at the same time, to become self-conscious cartographers. Summoning an anachronistic political geography, the accountants have moralized their location in a global environment by resorting to the old cold war geo-political map. They have formed an international body dominated by what they call the 'free-world nations'.[45] The resort to the geopolitical discourse of the cold war re-creates an external structure of antagonism while repressing structures of exclusion and antagonism within. The effect is to re-establish the comfortable illusion of objectivity that uniform national standards had supplied; the programme is one of harmonizing 'national standard-setting bodies', who are for them the significant global actors, in addition to the 'free world nations'.[46]

What is the effect of the accountant's new globalized self-under-standing? Whether operating nationally or extended globally, the world of investment and the management of money, viewed through the recent reflections of the accountancy profession, has the effect of conjuring away social, political, and ethical issues. It is a disconnected world in which structurally induced 'disadvantage' domestically and global inequality internationally cannot be discerned. For example, one of the issues of global standardization for accountants is differing approaches to the measurement of good will, where 'good will' is an accounting category. As a former head of the national accountancy standards committee has put it, for example, a primary issue is the 'useful life' of 'purchased good will'.[47] In Simmel's terms, with the rule of money, 'things become worn down and smoothed'.[48] and the accountancy profession has, in effect, hastened that smoothing pro-cess while, at the same time, deepening the repression of the ethical life.

This kind of repression is not peculiar to the discourse of account-ing. More generally, when the focus of one's approach to value is primarily on exchange value, the cultural predicates of value are repressed. Reflecting a pervasive tension, cultural practices tend to maintain the singularity of things, while commercial practices pro-mote their exchangeability. Historically, the tendency has been for commoditization to overcome cultural inhibition, especially in the industrialized and commercialized parts of the world. Nevertheless, different singularities hold in different places.[49] When cultural forces are heeded, it becomes clear that global difference involves structures of inhibition towards forms of exchange that cannot be harmonized by simply standardizing the language of accounting. Global difference is in part an expression of different patterns of commoditization. What is singular – that is, not exchangeable – is not susceptible to 'standardization' of commercial discourses. At issue, often, are in-commensurate cultural practices.

Not surprisingly, the discourse of US accounting is unreflective about the particularity of its cultural locus of enunciation and the different modalities of singularity that commercial practices encoun-ter. Insofar as there are expressions of ethical concern evinced by CPAs, they are doubtless related to the complicity of accounting with a relentless tendency for capitalist economies to be 'inherently re-sponsive to the pressure of commoditization', that is, 'to commoditize as widely as the exchange technology allows'.[50] Jonathan Crary has summarized this aspect of 'modernization' well; it is 'a process by which capitalism uproots and makes mobile what is grounded, clears away that which impedes circulation, and makes exchangeable what is singular'.[51]

This is particularly observable in the modern history of the industrialized parts of the world, where practices of singularity, for example, temporal domains of prohibition on commerce such as the keeping of a Sabbath by various religions, and spatial domains of prohibition on commercial exploitation such as the elementary school room, are overcome by the impetus to expand the domain of exchange. And apart from its impact on things, expanding capital relations – especially means through which the money form mediates relationships – transform social life by breaking down traditional forms of solidarity and provoking confrontations between ethical sensibilities and commercial practices.[52] While what might be an ethical response to such dynamics, at a domestic level, is controversial, at a minimum, it would involve more than supplying free consultation to those who cannot easily calculate the value of their location in this expanding world of commoditization.

The issue become more complex at the level of international and intercultural encounter. Because global capital flows create encounters between different life-worlds, even as they reconfigure them, at this level, 'good will', in the sense of an ethical posture towards a cultural Other, would involve a respect for that Other's practices of singularity and a recognition that 'otherness' is a dynamic, inextricably related to the way capital creates identity spaces. An elaborate concern with 'the ethical life' would necessitate both a recognition of the contingency of one's own identity as well as of the interdependencies of global relationships as they relate to structures of inequality. It is therefore propitious to inspect the globalization problematic of Christian ecumenicalists, for they have more experience adjusting moral reasoning to changes in global structures and dynamics.

Contemporary Christian Geography

The challenge of 'globalization' for Christian ecumenicalists, for whom 'the ethical life' is necessarily always foregrounded, is more conceptually encumbered and self-reflectively understood. Like the accounting profession, Christian ecumenicalists operate across a number of interdiscursive zones, but they do so with a much more variegated set of discursive genres; a globalized venue has always been part of their traditional self-understanding. Christian ecumenicalists have always aspired to a theology with global validity and have always explicitly recognized antagonism and resistance as constitutive of the structural demands on religious discourse.

The historical distinction between the discursive genres known as dogmatics and apologetics is predicated precisely on the disjunctive difference between believers inside and non-believers outside. For Christian ecumenicalists, the nation-state cartography, central to accountants (and of course primary for 'security' analysts), is less important than the pre-Westphalian religious map of believers versus non-believers. Moreover, their map contains a vertical dimension as well, extending from a sacred, transcendent domain downwards to a secular life-world. The mundane world, in which they draw the map of believers versus non-believers, is seen as divinely invested; it is shaped in part by 'the cunning hand of Providence' (as the theologian Max Stackhouse has put it in his theologized rendering of Hegel).[53] Christian ecumenicalists map a world in which theology and geography are combined, but of late that world seems increasingly resistant to an unambiguous mapping. It is 'globalization' that is the ambiguating force towards which some theologians are pointing.

Despite their long-held expectation of a global commitment, Christian ecumenicalists see a need to adjust to new forces reconfiguring the relationships between the local and the global. Treating what he calls 'the theological challenge of globalization', Stackhouse, for example, calls for a 'theological perspective large and supple enough truly to comprehend the social and religious pluralism of the globe'.[54] As is the case with CPAs, the perception is that globalization substitutes uncertainty and instability for the illusion of objectivity. As Stackhouse puts it:

> For those who have had little exposure to anything but a specific religious tradition or a denominational faith or a religion-saturated local or national culture, an introduction to world religions and to cosmopolitan cultures makes certainties less stable.[55]

The challenge of this new world of uncertainty, as 'believers' are confronted with an enforced 'deprovincialization', takes place within a distinctive perceptual mapping of the globe. While CPAs operate in a smoothed-out, financial world of (unfortunately) differential accounting standards, increasing the uncertainties for investment decisions, Christian ecumenicalists operate in a world of differential beliefs, which increases the uncertainties surrounding the production of kerygmatic (proclamatory) discourses.

Christian theologians have long recognized that their various genres of discourse: dogmatics, apologetics, and kerygmatics are haunted. Familiar with ghosts from the outset – they are constitutive of Christian spirituality – they have a long tradition of theorizing what is supposed to be fixed and enduring with respect to sources of value, while also recognizing that textual and proclamatory expressions of value are historically and linguistically contingent. For example, a committed deconstructionist could hardly improve upon this statement by a theologian of the paradoxes and uncertainties involved in moving from the dogmas of institutionalized scriptural interpretation to the injunctions of kerygmatic discourse:

> How can there be anything like dogma (which includes by definition the permanent, the lasting, the canonized in language), when historicity and linguistics have shown all language to be, despite any claim of the divine, quite human and always historical.[56]

Striving to overcome this seeming paradox, two theologians have sought to relocate the meaning of gospel 'truths' from the alleged historical origins of their inscriptions to the interface between what is inscribed and what is, at any time, theologically proclaimed. To warrant the move from the apostolic – what is already written in scriptures – to the kerygmatic – what is theologically uttered as regards the enduring truths of the apostolic (received) truth – they suggest that revelation is not sufficiently realized in mere inscription. Revelation becomes actualized only when it is proclaimed. The truth of the Gospels, by this account, is relocated in the 'interplay' of text and proclamation.[57]

However persuasive the effects of such philosophical/ theological work on 'communities of believers' may be, the practice of Christian theology has required for its coherence an energetic, forthright confrontation with the ghosts of contingency immanent in the establishment of non-contingency. What have been less self-reflectively attended to in theological discourse are the boundary issues surrounding the primary Christian constituency, the 'community of believers'. *Its* coherence and demarcation is a necessary condition for, among other things, the very distinction between dogmatics and apologetics.

The issue of the community of believers is precisely what disrupts the recent encounter of Christian ecumenicalism with globalization. Consolidating the Christian 'we' as 'communities of faith', for example, Stackhouse urges a resistance to 'ethnocentrism in faith' and a corresponding attention to 'comparative religion'.[58] Two significant repressions are involved in these suggestions. The first, which constructs a 'community of faith' effectively denies an ongoing history of disagreement and schism within Christianity. The second, which constructs non-Christian religious alterity as 'ethnic', or (as is used later) as 'cultural', effectively denies the pan-ethnic and transcultural bases of other religions. This latter repression has a hoary tradition. During its earliest encounters with Islam in the ancient world and continuing through the Renaissance, Christian writers avoided using religious markers for Muslims and instead referred to them in ethnic terms: as Saracens, Moors, Tatars, among others.[59]

Although beliefs rather than ethnicities have been the target of Christian ecumenicalists, the ethnic form of address has served historically to diminish the validity of the belief systems of the non-Christian Other. Accordingly, the general thrust of the speculation on the implications of globalization is towards compassion but not towards an ultimate acceptance of a non-believing alterity or a permission for others to remain enigmatic within the conceits of Christendom. The world's subjects are enclosed within a rigorously drawn moral cartography; conceptual mastery is the necessary strategy, but the tactics must shift. It is ultimately necessary for all to participate in 'a common life' but persuasion must be other than merely a matter of the exercise of the traditional 'dogmatic method', appropriate to 'those who already (or almost) believe'. What is now needed is 'the apologetic method', appropriate when entering 'into philosophical and cultural-linguistic systems other than our own', when making a 'substantive case for that which we hold to be true in the face of those who really do not know, and cannot imagine, what we are talking about'.[60]

The sharp distinction between dogmatic and apologetic methods works together with the grammatical consolidations (the 'we's', 'our's') to construct a united community of believers, who face a world of ideational division while repressing division within. A return to the historical period roughly corresponding to late antiquity, when Christianity was taking shape in opposition to various alternative spiritualities and cosmologies, takes us back as well to a beginning of a history of repression within Christianity.

In the fifth century, Christianity elaborated a mythic secular history, a story of Christianization in which Christianity rapidly and wholly displaced paganism in 'Christendom'. However, historical experience is recalcitrant to this narrative. Rather than producing a radical departure from paganism, Christianity shared its stage. As Peter

Brown has pointed out, the public culture of ruling elites in the age of Constantine did not represent themselves in terms of Christian but rather in terms of pagan cosmology: on the mosaics in their villas and the ceremonial icons in the imperial court, as well as in poetic and letter-writing styles.[61] Moreover, throughout the fifth century, rather than an unambiguous Christianization, Christianity and paganism worked together in public representations – in maps and calendars for example. To the extent that a Christian world imaginary displaced a pagan one, the shift was not rapid: 'the ancient representation of the *mundus* was one which shifted with the slowness of a glacier'.[62]

As a result, the Christian imaginary never shed much of its link with paganism. There were strenuous attempts to avoid what Christians regarded as the polluting effects of pagan practices, especially blood sacrifice, but in the ancients' "though-worlds", potentially exclusive explanatory systems coexisted'.[63] However complete or partial was the separation of Christian doctrine from paganism – complete if one heeds only authorized Christian narratives but partial if one heeds ethno-historical scholarship – the challenge of Islam, since its beginning in the seventh century, has constituted a far more significant challenge to Christianity's distinctiveness.

Bernard Lewis has put the matter simply: 'Compared with the remoter cults and culture of Asia and Africa, Islam and Christianity are sister religions, with an immense shared heritage.' [64] Both aspire to a truth that is valid for all human kind, and both absorbed Jewish commitments to monotheism, prophecy, revelation and scripture, Greek philosophy and science, and Roman law and patterns of governance.[65] Certainly the two religions departed in terms of their foundation myths, but their sharing of local vernaculars made a fairly direct encounter, on comparable terms, possible. As Lewis notes, 'those medieval monks who translated the Qur'an into Latin in order to refute it were able to do so because Latin, by that time a Christian language, had the necessary terms'.[66] And perhaps most significantly, both Christianity and Islam incorporate 'Jewish scriptures', although in different ways. For Christianity, Judaism was incomplete and for Islam it was false.[67]

Muslim and Christian, like Arab (or Canaanite) and Jew, have striven to separate themselves in the face of the disquieting suspicion that their similarities and shared origins are more significant than their differences. In the case of ancient Jewish doctrine, the striving took the form of dire warnings by Israelite prophets about the corrupting influence of Canaanite ritual, for example the sexual, drinking cults of the Baal worshipers, those whom, Jeremiah claimed, have 'assembled themselves by troops in harlots' houses' (Jeremiah 5:7). In the case of Christian doctrine, much of the literature known as apologetics (a tradition evoked in Stackhouse's injunction to approach global pluralism with apologetic rather than dogmatic method) has historically been aimed at Islam.[68]

While the apologetics of early Christians were vociferous and uncompromising about the location of 'truth', contemporary Christian ecumenicalists have adopted a softer version of apologetics for a globalized age. Stackhouse insists, nevertheless, that contemporary apologetics must confront Others with a knowledge of how their doctrines specifically mislead. But resisting the unreflective coherence that his 'we' and 'our' grammar implies, he evinces a recognition that Christianity in 'America' was shaped by various different 'strands': Roman and anti-Roman, Protestant, and reformist, for example.[69]

Once these different strands are acknowledged, however, they become symbiotic for purposes of producing an apologetics aimed outwards. The Protestant dimension helps to construct arguments suited to 'debunking false claims to universality in the name of particularity', and the reformist dimension helps in 'the recovery and actualization of a vision of eternal truth'.[70] What finally emerges is a 'theological community' ready to deliver an apologetic to convince those who fail to know or imagine what Christians are talking about.[71] The different strands become articulated once the ecumenical gaze recovers its outward focus.

Yet Christian ecumenicalists remain haunted by schisms in the ideational coherence they had ascribed to Christendom. As one theologian has noted, contemporary apologetics must confront a 'breakdown of certainties' within, produced by the migration of 'historical-critical methods', 'feminist criticism', 'Marxist analysis', and 'black studies', all of which point to 'long obscured realities', and produce a 'confusion' in the study of Christian theology.[72] Although the writer does not put it in these terms, the challenges to Christian doctrine within – like a recognition of the historical entanglements between Christian and other doctrines – disrupt the very distinction between a dogmatic and apologetic method. Ignoring this disruption, Christian ecumenicalists have urged a 'clarity' about what doctrine is and undertaken a new mapping of the global venues of non-belief.[73] These reactions to the perceived inadequacies of Christian ecumenical discourse, like those of the accounting profession, can provide some insights into the discursive adjustments of security analysts. Making this case requires yet another leap into the past; the homologies can be made apparent once they are located within a temporal montage.

Performing National History

The discursive aporias expressed by the accounting profession in reaction to the 'globalization' phenomenon operate within roughly the same imagined world as that of the security analyst. It is a geopolitical world separating the 'free world' (or the West) from the rest. And the ideological repressions are markedly similar. There is, not surprisingly, no robust consideration of what is unfree (or even non-West) within the West, much less an elaborated acknowledgement of the ways that the way of life in 'the West' influences how people are able to live – for example, the dangers they face and the forms of work they can find – outside of it.

The relationship between Christian ecumenicalist and security discourses invites more profound comparison. What are especially comparable are the struggles, manifested in both the histories of Christianity and in secular theorizing of post-Westphalian states, individually or as part of a state system, to consolidate conceptually and morally their domains of operation. Their contemporary approaches to the production of their imaginaries and the narratives that support them began to emerge in roughly the same period. The structural changes producing both state and contemporary Christian problematics begin, according to Foucault, in the sixteenth century when there was an:

> intersection of two processes: the process which, shattering the structures of feudalism, is about to form the great territorial, administrative and colonial states; and . . . a totally different movement which, starting with the Reformation and then the Counter-Reformation, put in question the manner in which one is to be spiritually ruled and led on this earth in order to achieve eternal salvation.[74]

The shaping of state space greatly affected the nature of the more or less continuous hermeneutic performance through which Christianity, despite its supposition that Christian doctrine is predicated on enduring and revealed truths, has approached the consolidation and maintenance of its domain.[75] To maintain the stability of its imaginary – a map that includes a transcendent domain plus a mundane world of believers and non-believers, now divided on the basis of national as well as spiritual loyalties – theologians have altered the focus of their interpretive struggles. Perhaps the earliest interpretive adjustment was undertaken by Saint Paul, who strove to supercede Christianity's Jewish origins and to challenge textual authority by radically distinguishing 'spirit' and 'letter'.[76] The more recent problem is an attempt to cope with an expanding global pluralism, which, as noted, is seen as requiring a resuscitation of the apologetic method.

Doubtless, it is difficult to reconcile the 'Cunning of Providence' with the divine permissiveness implied in the proliferation of non-truth (as Christians ecumenicalists construe an increasing global diversity). It may have been easier to accept a model of a more or less Christianized West in competition with an atheistic East than to come to terms with a non-West that is, at the same time, a non-East emerging into clearer focus. Christianity's doctrinal resources have been more suited to the former global polarity. Nevertheless, whatever the historical challenge, an active theorizing (or perhaps better: theologizing) has been deployed to maintain the stability of the Christian imaginary while, at the same time, hoping for its expansion into a Christian oikumene.

Security analysts are perhaps the most steadfast representatives of another historical interpretive performance. Their story of modernity is one in which the European style of 'nation-state' with a capitalist economy is represented as the highest form of political achievement and in which threats to political security have involved, at one juncture, other kinds of states and, at present, transnational forms of political initiative (for example Islamic political movements) as well. It's time to highlight the issue of geo-political security.

'Security'

In their recent articulations, as security analysts seek to map what they see as present global dangers, the imagined cultural unity of the American nation is extended to a more general cultural unity ascribed to 'the West'. In this regard, Samuel Huntington's version of this new mapping, his notion of the present 'clash of civilizations',[77] is particularly worthy of scrutiny. However before responding to Huntington's approach to globalization and its dangers, it is important to treat more generally what Jameson has referred to as the process of collapsing ontology with geography, especially as it is evident in security-oriented global mappings in general.[78]

Two approaches to the self-recognition of the modern state help to situate this issue. First, it is necessary to heed what Michael Taussig has called 'the cultural practice of statecraft',[79] in which the state is understood to be continually crafting itself as the avatar of a national culture. Second, it is necessary to locate the ways in which that cultural practice of the state constructs the worlds of danger to its coherence.

This latter aspect of the state's structures of self-recognition and reproduction is most evident in security discourses. 'Security' is not a thing to be defined, indeed as a concept among scholars of international politics it is more or less 'essentially contested';[80] it is to be understood in terms of how and when it is articulated. While its articulation is often associated with strategic arguments in struggles among states, it is also expressed as part of the general ontological defence of the primacy of the state and its claim to be supported by and expressive of a primordial sovereign/citizen identity.

Construed in this way, 'security' emerges as involvement in the ontological grounding of the political.[81] Such grounding in stabilizing performances, as they have operated within the dominant state system, have had two dimensions, usefully distinguished by Jens Bartelson. 'Security', he notes 'divides every state ontologically from every other form of political organization by presenting everything that is prior in time or external in space as a threat.'[82] One could add, by summoning a genre of Christian discourse, that this aspect of the state's performance constitutes much of its dogma. Unlike the agonistic map invented by those who shaped the imaginary of Christendom, however, states resist recognizing that they live in a world of non-believers. While Christianity explicitly named and addressed competitors, state discourses (in some ways Huntington's version is an exception) conjure them away, for example locating non-state or non-sovereign peoples in discourses of deviance, lawlessness, or terrorism.

States effectively extend their dogmatic method by participating in what Bartelson identifies as the second aspect of state practices of sovereignty: rituals of mutual recognition. He suggests that states rely for their coherence on reputation, the recognition accorded to them as states by other states.[83] This gives rise to various acts of reciprocal recognition, even by states who are involved in violent conflicts. The politics of security – the politics of securing the grounds of the political by locating it exclusively in the territorialized identities of states – takes the form of a politics of identity. To be coherent, to become what Bartelson calls being general unto itself,[84] the state constructs itself as a discrete and completed entity with respect to other states, not individually but other states taken as a whole; this constitutes the 'outside' of the state as contrasted with its sovereign inside.[85]

Bartelson's tale of state sovereignty, its practices of security and reputation, more or less reflects the security preoccupations of security analysts focused on interactions within the world of states. The politics of security for this profession has been nothing less than the reproduction of a state-oriented cosmology that conjures away extra-state attachments and articulations which share their times and spaces, very much the way that Christian discourse, since the age of Constantine, has repressed gnostic and pagan attachments and expressions, by allowing them no recognition within doctrinal discourses.[86]

With this as a preface, we can continue with the temporal montage and bring into focus once again the articulated anxieties of the contemporary security analyst, Samuel Huntington, who mistakes his ontological and cosmological commitments to a geo-political and civilizational order for a detached, realist assessment of threats to the 'security' of the 'West'. Failing to see the arbitrariness in the relationships between civilizational codes and their referents, he sees other 'civilizations' as relatively stable phenomena that are external security threats to the West, and he views the immigration of non-Western Others as internal threats to what he constructs as a unitary American national culture.

Huntington's 'Clash of Civilizations'

Huntington's recent rethinking of the structure of global competition is doubtless spurred by globalization trends as well as the dissolving of the old cold war cartography. He, like others functioning within various different sectors of the social domain, decided to rethink the national collective identity in the face of more rapid movements of people, commodities, and money, and an increasingly rapid dissemination of ideas that have challenged traditional forms of global consciousness.[87] Persons in various parts of the social domain are rethinking themselves and their worlds, and, for a security analyst, what has emerged is a new version of the configuration of planetary threats.

To appreciate Huntington's mode of worlding, one has to know how he approaches maps at a meta level. Ironically, despite being one who uses power as a dominant category for interpreting global process, Huntington views knowledge as primarily technical; appropriately pursued, it has no intimacy with the operation of power or authority. He suggests that maps simply serve a rational, heuristic function:

Simplified paradigms or maps are indispensable for human thought and action . . . We need explicit or implicit models to: 1. Order and generalize about reality; 2. understand causal relationships among phenomena; 3. anticipate and, if we are lucky, predict future developments; 4. distinguish what is important from what is unimportant; and 5. show us what paths we should take to achieve our goals.[88]

In contrast, over a century ago Joseph Conrad understood well the 'violence of representation' that is a part of some geographic imaginaries.[89] Under the general rubric of 'imperial geography', he proposed a chronology of geographic perspectives that accompanied and legitimated various stages in the process of the European colonization. His stages ran from 'geography fabulous', based on myths of the new world, through 'geography militant', coinciding with the 'invasions', to 'geography triumphant', expressed in the subsequent cartographic representations of the European settlements.[90] As Conrad's discussion makes clear, maps reflect practised imaginaries; they are irredeemably entangled with moral and political projects.[91] The 'power–knowledge' circuit that Conrad's 'geography triumphant' reflected was associated with the establishment of the Euro-American-dominated geo-political world of states. Huntington's replacement of that map with one based on a civilizational ordering reflects another project. Rather than extending the early project of settlement and domination, it is a project of enclavization, of retreating to the citadel of 'Western civilization' around which he draws a line that separates the West from 'the rest'.

To proceed in Conrad's spirit and challenge Huntington's disinterested model of cartography, it is necessary to locate geo-political cartographies in a temporal structure, displacing Huntington's current map with a mobilizing cartographic time image. The current, radical instability of the security oriented map – the maps of global danger (to the United States or to 'the West') drawn in different ways by different security analysts – reflects the prior stability of the old cold war map, a practical and moral geography, featuring the antagonism between the United States/NATO and the 'East bloc', and a separate array of 'Third World' nations committed to either neutrality or to varying degrees of partisanship with respect to the two competing blocs. To understand that which security seeks to secure, which is increasingly articulated as cultural and civilizational, it is necessary to examine earlier cartographies. A genealogy of political space, which treats impulses ranging from Roman ecumenicalism to early and later periods of nation-building can help us resist the naturalizing of geo-political space that has been characteristic of analysts who treat only the recent history of international antagonism.

'The first maps in western history', according to Claude Nicolet, appeared during the Persian War and were shaped by the attempts at 'visualizations of the distances that were destined to mark, or to mask, the balance of power'.[92] Accordingly, Strabo's maps articulated the Roman view of the world and the place within it that the ecumenically inclined Romans had assigned themselves.[93] Inasmuch as Strabo's maps were also expressions, more specifically, of Caesar Augustus's ecumenical conception of the Roman Empire, there was a significant entanglement between Caesar's in-process autobiography and the geography of empire. The world represented was the one that Augustus meant to master. Subsequently, however, biography and cartography parted company. By the Renaissance, the geo-politics represented by official cartographers in 'the West' began to indicate a separation from the imprimaturs of emperors and monarchs. In England, for example, cartographic representations had begun to diminish the space formerly assigned to 'insignia of royal power', which had reflected identities based on 'dynastic loyalty', and increasingly emphasized markers of land configuration and national territory.[94]

By the seventeenth century, the succession of images on maps reflected a historical sequence 'from universal Christendom, to dynastic state, to land-centered nation.'[95] Contrary to Kant's radical separation between history, or narrative and geography, subsequent western cartography has been significantly shaped by stories of encounter. If, for example, we jump ahead to the period of nation building in the eighteenth century it becomes clear that 'the text of geography is not an innocent one'.[96] Eighteenth-century travel writers were lending a story of cultural encounter to the emerging geo-political map. The writings of Thomson and Chateaubriand, among others, reflected a commitment to secure the 'home', the national space of their respective 'Western' nations in the face of encounters with exotic Others.[97]

This tradition of securing the home, whether the space of the nation or 'western civilization' more generally, has been reflected in the convergence of geographic imaginaries and the security mentality in the west ever since. But the civilizational dimension of this mentality has its own historical trajectory. To challenge this dimension of the Huntington cartography, it is necessary to create a temporal rather than static image of 'civilization', for while the old, realist Huntington focused primarily on states, the new civilizational Huntington focuses on cultural rather than geo-political clashes within a 'world order' he sees as civilizational rather than nation-state based:

> The world is in some sense two, but the central distinction is between the West as the hitherto dominant civilization and all the others, which, however, have little if anything in common among them. The world, in short, is divided between a Western one and a non-Western many.[98]

The most dangerous civilizational challenge for Huntington is 'Islam'. While it has been convincingly shown that despite a resurgence of orthodox Islamic religious commitments, contemporary Islam harbors a complex and pluralistic set of relationships between religious and political institutions,[99] Huntington's Islam is constituted as a 'global religious revival'.[100] The civilizational coherence that Huntington is seeking to protect from Islam is a historical construction that has taken shape in different ways at different times, but, at present, it is connected to a perspective, reproduced by Huntington, that emerged in the past two centuries. Whereas the absolute monarchies were concerned with ruling their 'subjects', the modern state legitimated itself in terms of the alleged cultural unity of its population.

Since the late eighteenth century, the 'governmentality'[101] of the European state has increasingly oriented state practices towards managing various social and cultural dynamics. Indeed part of the state's control over the meaning of the political has involved it in 'the capture of cultural identity'.[102] Forces such as demographic expansion, monetary abundance, and agricultural growth, encouraged governments to turn to the problem of managing an economy and to 'security', the policing of the boundaries within which this management of people in relation to things was to take place. They became preoccupied, at least in the European case, with the 'population . . . as the ultimate end of government'.[103] Ultimately, this preoccupation resulted, from at least the mid nineteenth century, in high levels of surveillance of sexual and other practices that moralists associate with the maintenance of 'decency', so that the nation's 'public sphere' is the place where 'decent' or 'civilized' behaviour is to take place. Throughout its modern history, nationalism and codes of decency have been significantly interrelated.[104] Its more recent interarticulations have been evident in campaigns of those associated with saving 'American civilization' against sexually explicit media.

In a recent piece in the editional pages of the *New York Times*, for example, William Bennett and C. Deloris Tucker praised the Wal-Mart store chain for refusing to stock 'compact disks with lyrics and cover art that it finds objectionable'[105] and appealed for 'simple decency', which they claim has the support of 'concerned parents and politicians of both parties'.[106] To connect this concern with maintaining decency by policing media with a security problematic, it is necessary to recognize the interrelationships between 'decency' as a dimension of cultural evaluation and the historical emergence of the idea of 'civilization'. Although both decency and civilizational codes were initially employed within European societies, they became associated eventually with the impetus to nationalism and thus to national distinctiveness in the world of states. The entanglement between domestic and international concerns certainly remains. To protect the bourgeois culture of decency, which Bennett and others associate with 'American' culture, for example, they and others evoke the idea of the American civilization.

Clearly, those who summon civilizational and cultural codes and attach them to the practices of 'western' nations see them as both self-evident and as signs of distinction. But a historical perspective on the emergence of these codes of judgement reveals that what are now regarded as unproblematic styles of behaviour and affect – especially patterns of inhibition versus release of emotion and physical violence – are a product of a slow historical shaping process since the middle ages. And, even during the twentieth century, significant changes in affective patterns are in evidence: for example the change from drinking in the workplace to a situation of workplace sobriety and leisure sphere inebriation.[107]

In Europe, civilité' as a guide to behaviour developed concurrently with state formation. In the 'age of absolutism', it was associated with the processes through which western societies imposed domestic pacification. While the behaviours were being shaped, there developed a concurrent concept of civilization which was to become part of European self-appreciation, although in different states, that civilizational discourse took on different qualities and was differently connected to antagonisms between classes.[108] Most significantly, the norms prescribing constraints and codes of decency, which initially related primarily to within society class dynamics as well as to state-sponsored aspect of pacification, acquired a collective, ontological significance; they became part of a cluster of ideas about national distinctiveness. George Mosse argues that the norms comprising civilité' needed a broader warrant; they 'had to be informed by an ideal if they were to be effective . . . In most timely fashion, nationalism came to the rescue.'[109] And since the epoch of state-formation, in which these codes and nationalism have been interconnected, the civilizational map has served various expressions of domestic anxiety about dangers to the nation and/or to western civilization as a whole.

Currently, although the civilizational discourse has been evident primary in attempts to distinguish the 'West' from the rest, different defenders of the cultural decency and civilizational particularity of 'American people' draw different maps. In a recent obscenity case before a US federal court, for example, danger to the decency of American cultural practices was associated with the licentious sexuality of French and Brazilians. An appellate judge involved in a case brought against a bar with nude dancing in South Bend, Indiana, said: 'We may doubt the wisdom of requiring women to wear more clothing in the bars of South Bend than in the *Folies Bergère* or on the beaches of Rio de Janeiro without concluding that Indiana has exceeded its powers under the Constitution.'[110] Another dimension of the moral geography of obscenity law emerged in a related case, when in *Miller* v. *Civil City of South Bend*, the court judged the Indiana statute barring nude dancing unconstitutional. In his support of the decision, Judge Posner evoked the image of 'Islamic Clergy' whom, he added, 'most of us do not admire', acting as a 'morals police patrolling the streets of South Bend with knouts, like the Saudis'.[111]

Modernity in western nations is therefore a period in which we witness the coalescence of the codes of civilization and decency. Historically, the triumph of the bourgeois classes has been associated with their specific codes of decency. Added to that since then, however, has been the post hoc moralizing of those codes which has allowed them to be a basis for judgement of both deviance within the state and dangers from without. As a result, the modern state has in various ways performed its commitment to possessing a distinctive national culture. And in an age when some aspects of state authority are attenuated, new performances are summoned – for example the cultural festival, which has taken on a greater sense of urgency:

> In an era when global extension and international flows of capital and information, along with forces of separatism, have made 'the nation' seem like a threatened species, national cultural festivals are a very particular sign of the repackaging of the imagery of that political entity.[112]

Huntington's attempt to consolidate a cultural singularity for the United States and 'the West' constitutes another form of repackaging.

It is a form of secular kerygmatics, an attempt to proclaim a unity in the face of a diversity that cannot be conjured away. As Étienne Balibar has noted, 'No nation, that is no national state, has an ethnic basis . . . but they do have to institute in real (and therefore in historical) time their imaginary unity *against* other possible unities.'[113] In order to produce such an imaginary unity, Huntington must freeze-frame culture. His fear of an assault on Western culture requires a static version of 'culture', which he construes as a more or less fixed civilizational characteristic, based primarily on mentalities – for example 'shared beliefs'.[114]

If one focuses instead on dynamics of acculturation, it becomes difficult to fix either 'American' or 'western' culture. Over time, 'culture' in the sense of practices of space, memory, subjectivity, and collective responsibility (among other things), alters as various different peoples share proximity as well as engaging in both direct and mediated encounters. What has produced 'western civilization' has been a dynamic of adjustment as various cultural practices, often attributed to the non-West, inflect 'western' cultural practices. Moreover, and significantly, what are largely responsible for the production of spaces of association, perhaps the major condition of possibility for modern culture and the encounters that construct and reconstruct it, are changes in the production, accumulation and marketing of consumable goods.

But Huntington conjures away the effects of political economy in his story of cultural coherence and his construction of a threatened coherence: 'western civilization'. His discourse on culture fails to register the economic predicates of its mobility. What some call 'culture' is in part an effect of the interaction of cultural and economic practices. Cultural encounter and change, or, perhaps better, dynamics of acculturation, are owed in large part to changes in global political economy.[115] Cultural practices both constitute and are constituted by changes in economy that are not contained by the boundaries of states or 'civilizations'.

Huntington's security-oriented mapping of civilizations focuses on identity commitments, but, at the same time, conjures away the effects of capital on the production of selves. Certainly one can make a rough distinction between the western, individualized or ego-oriented self and that of traditional societies in which identity is related less to an individual's projects and more to a cosmological structure of authority that submerges the individual in a collective social network that understands itself in relation to that cosmology.[116] But such differences should not be overstated, because the nation as a symbolic imaginary serves very much like a traditional religion's cosmology, and capital accumulations and flows, or more generally the dynamics of global capital, are as responsible for identity spaces as are the historical traditions one can group within such civilizational domains as Islam or 'the West'.

Although, in various ways, Huntington's security-oriented mapping is forgetful of political economy, capitalism haunts his analysis without being named. The map of exchanges radically ambiguates any attempt to draw rigid lines around peoples, nations or civilizations and it disrupts an attempt at locating motives or intentions causally within any geographic domain. Revealingly, for example, Huntington constructs the goals of the 'West' as: (1) maintaining military superiority; (2) promoting western values and institutions; and (3) gaining the respect of others for basic human rights. To contest this model of objectives, one need point to no more than the way pressures from various commercial enterprises have often trumped either security interests or a concern for Western values or human rights in producing the radically inconsistent pressures the United States has placed on various other states' human rights policies (for example, harassing Havana and tolerating Korean and Chinese restrictions).

Huntington conveniently neglects the imbrications between security and economy. He does not, for example, note the way that his civilizational map, a structure of civilizational 'fault lines', is transected and thus violated by the West's pattern of arms trading, which is often inconsistent with several of the 'goals of the West' that he celebrates. But given the current situation of US military hegemony, Huntington is doubtless less worried about the flow of arms than the flow of people. Global political economy, still dominated by 'the West', has the primary responsibility for the current changes in the US ethnoscape. Huntington's reactions to these changes relate more to his preoccupation with 'cultural' than military security. However, to construct the problematic of cultural security, Huntington must effect what is his most significant conjuring act; he must construct a model of a consensual and more or less exclusive culture in order to have it threatened by global trends.

Certainly, Huntington recognizes that capital flows are implicated in people flows, but his argument about the problem with the changing US ethnoscape is defended by locating the immigration issues in the domain of public opinion. The political issue of protecting one's cultural singularity then becomes a matter of implementing restrictions that comport with a population's attitudes. Apart from neglecting the diasporic identities within such 'populations,' Huntington never addresses for example the duplicity involved in a symbolic politics that disparages illegal immigration (about which one can evoke negative attitudes) and a fiscal politics that brings no pressure to bear on businesses that exploit a cheap immigrant workforce.[117]

In addition to conjuring away political economy, Huntington conjures away the foreignness within 'the West'. This is not the place to treat his various oversimplifications and depluralizations of the so-called non-West. A critical literature has increasingly addressed these shortcomings.[118] It is his geographic imaginary, his practice of line-drawing that one must address to recognize how Huntington, and indeed the security analyst in general, manages to conceptually isolate what is ambiguous with respect to civilizational groupings.

In constructing a 'fortress community'[119] by drawing lines between the West and the rest, Huntington denies the interdependencies involved in producing and reproducing the West and the rest, as well as the ambiguities of the cultural orientations within the various groupings. The consequences of this kind of boundary fixation can be demonstrated with reference to the retrospective treatment of one source of the barbarian anxiety that those who worry about 'cultural security' manifest, the story of the fall of ancient Rome.

Contrary to the familiar story of the fall of ancient Rome – that it succumbed to the barbarians at the gates – Rome could not be understood as circumscribed by sharp boundaries. As C. R. Whittaker has shown, Roman frontiers were not precise lines of defence or enforcement, which radically separated what was Rome from non-Rome. Roman frontiers were more zonal than wall-like.[120] The ancient world had been, in varying degrees, Romanized, and the place between Rome and non-Rome was a zone, not a wall of defence. Nevertheless, one contemporary security analyst, relying on the mythic, barbarians at the gates story and preoccupied with modern geo-political lines, succumbed to the temptation to see Rome in terms of strict geo-political boundaries rather than ambiguous zonal frontiers.[121]

In like manner, Huntington has drawn a sharp boundary around 'western culture'. In order to do so, he too must rely on an ethnographically dubious story, one about the development of 'the West'. His emphasis is on the establishment of a harmonious and consensual order rather than on, for example, the struggles that remain within the order. While he ethnicizes the conflicts abroad, based on mythic histories of such global arenas as the Balkans, which never had the sharp ethnic divisions that he and other security analysts ascribe to them,[122] he de-ethnicizes the western peoplescapes and constructs the civilization of the West on the basis of abstract principles such as 'equality before the law'. Ironically, this abstract principle, perhaps more than any other, is violated by much of the history of the West. From the initial assaults on indigenous peoples in the Americas – who have no places on Huntington's map – through the unequal treatment of peoples of African origin, to the current treatment of both legal and non-legal immigrants, the story of 'the West' is a story of practices of radical exclusion, followed by slow and grudging acceptance or domestication of foreignness within at the level of juridical identification and protection while at the level of the mythologizing of western freedom, it is a denial of those practices of exclusion.

To hark back to the discursive economies of Christian discourse, we could say that there is a radical confusion of security analysts' dogmatics and apologetics. In assuming that 'the West' (like Christendom) has been secured as a wholly separate identity, they see only a need for a dogmatics. But unlike the current posture of the Christian ecumenicalists, the security orientation now uttered by Huntington against the threat of Islam, has given up on apologetics. An Islam, which is radically depluralized in Huntington's discourse, is represented as impervious to western doctrine, however articulated. Thus Huntington attempts to achieve the coherence of the West by radically abjecting the Other (for example, Islam) as outside and incommensurate. The radical difference that Huntington ascribes to warring parties in the Balkans, for example,[123] is such a projection. There are no cultural or civilizational essences to be found inside or outside, only dynamic relationships that achieve a seeming essence only to the degree that they are fixed in the discursive practices through which specific projects of identity/difference are mobilized.

The identity/difference practice for the security analyst, then, is haunted by time. Only by momentarily fixing what constantly changes can one found, in one's imagination, *a* culture or *a* civilization.[124] The particular configuration that Huntington thinks he discerns outside the West owes more to his freeze-framing than to the world on which his vision is imposed. And most significantly, Huntington's mode of discrete temporality is accompanied by a mode of thinking space that is dogmatic. Mistaking his moral geography – the abjection of various forms of otherness outside of West and the denial of otherness within it – for perspicuous knowledge, he thinks that his way of thinking has stable and unproblematic referents, that it allows him to 'order and generalize about reality'.[125]

The 'reality' that Huntington assembles in his West versus the rest mapping of the globe constitutes a moral geography, a security-oriented ethico-political initiative aimed at protecting an enclave whose civilizational integrity is a more a function of the way he tells the story of modernity than it is of discernable cultural or civilizational difference. And, as a neo-Kantian, one who radically separates geography from the construction of history, Huntington sees his maps as wholly innocent of ethical and political commitment.

Different Heading

Ethical self-reflection becomes possible when negotiation with difference rather than security is the project, and when thought is seen in terms of normative performance rather than referential adequacy. It is possible and desirable to think a more hospitable world, one that welcomes encounter with difference rather than securing identity.[126] Towards this end, we can consider Jacques Derrida's alternative story of the constitution of 'the West'. Apart from his commitment to global hospitality, in which he sees Europe's responsibility as one of recognizing the debt of 'European civilization' to the non-western other, Derrida, like Kant, is attuned to the power of examples and the importance of reading the signs of the times. Unlike Kant, however, Derrida is not unambiguously sanguine about what he sees:

> Hope, fear, and trembling are commensurate with the signs that are coming to us from everywhere in Europe, where, precisely in the name of identity, be it cultural or not, the worst violences those that we recognize all too well without yet having thought them through, the crimes of xenophobia, racism, anti-Semitism, religious or nationalist fanaticism, are being unleashed, mixed up, mixed up with each other, but also, and their is nothing fortuitous in this, mixed in with the breath, with the respiration, with the very 'spirit' of promise.[127]

Also, unlike Kant, Derrida sees geography in general and the Western or European geographic imaginary in particular as thoroughly entangled with a story/history that has been radically inhospitable: 'In its physical geography, and in what has often been called, its *spiritual geography*, Europe has always recognized itself as a cape or headland.'[128]

Derrida's reads contemporary signs as one who is much less comfortable than was Kant in being able to utter 'we' when locating himself on the European continent.[129] Describing himself as 'a sort of over-acculturated, over-colonized European hybrid,'[130] it is not insignificant that Derrida, who has a diasporic identity, wants Europe to 'invent another gesture',[131] to resist its historical tendency to regard itself as exemplary and to take a more responsible and hospitable posture with respect to 'other headings', by which (in a Kantian, cosmopolitan spirit) he wants Europe to imagine an open future in which one cannot expect to be able to read the world by sacrilizing and radically securing its own borders.

Interestingly, Derrida and Huntington are in agreement that the West should no longer take itself as a universal exemplar. What most radically distinguishes their reactions to this realization are the political initiatives they derive. While Huntington opts for an enclave strategy, aimed at securing the West's civilizational coherence, Derrida wants 'the West' to open itself to a different self-understanding, one in which it recognizes its own discordances and inconsistencies, the incoherences that follow all its attempts at imposing coherence. In short, a hospitality to alterity, for Derrida, must be predicated on a hospitality to oneself, to a recognition of difference within.

And, finally, both Derrida and Huntington resist the politics of closure in the end of history argument (both are critical of Fukuyama's triumph of the liberal-capitalism model), but ultimately Huntington seeks, through his concern with security, a politics of closure, a politics aimed at securing identity through a fixing of the territoriality of 'the West' as a coherent collectivity. In contrast, Derrida's politics is specifically a politics of non-closure. He constructs the political task not as one of securing boundaries but of 'the reinvention of political concepts to measure up to the technicalization and globalization of political communities in the next century'.[132] This requires, among other things, a resistance to 'national-philosophism', which is 'the claim laid by one country or nation to the privilege of "representing", "embodying", "identifying with", the universal essence of man, the thought of which is supposedly produced in some way in the philosophy of that people of that nation'.[133]

Conclusion: Unsecuring through Uncommon Sense

Derrida's elaboration of Kant's critical recognition of the limits of conceptuality was no doubt deepened by the territorial ambiguities of his identity. His 'reinventions of political concepts' and resistance to 'national philosophism' are spurred and enabled by his diasporic experience as a Europeanized Algerian and his resulting profound ambivalence towards his affiliation with Euro-western space and the Euro-oriented story of modernity. Diasporic intellectuals are intervening and repoliticizing a variety of historical and contemporary domains of inquiry, bringing to the task of ethico-political critique perspectives based on non-traditional territorial experiences.[134] For example, the Argentine literary scholar Walter Mignolo attributes his alternative reading of the Renaissance to his experience as a son of Italian immigrants, living in a 'predominantly Spanish nation' and dealing with the 'fusion of horizons' between the canonical tradition of Spanish literary culture and its present manifestation in the work of Latin-American literary scholars.[135] Designating his interpretive orientation as a 'pluritopic hermeneutics', he focuses on 'the politics of enacting and . . . constructing loci of enunciation', which must necessarily introduce ethical issues into knowledge problematics.[136]

Mignolo's pluritopic hermeneutics is not simply a version of multi-culturalism, that is of a recognition that alternative perspectives on reality obtain. Rather, it recognizes that the enactments involved in producing interpretations issue from selves that cannot be unambiguously located in space. The politics of interpretation becomes not a matter of countenancing the perspectives of alternative cultural actors but of destabilizing the very relationship between space and enunciation. Within such a politics, one substitutes for territorial stability as the predicate for the production of meaning, an interacting plurality of meaning performances issuing from a map that is always in a situation of becoming.

Much of the critical force of Mignolo's work derives from the complex process of territorial becoming to which his biography attests. He experiences a continual ambiguity between what might be his 'homeland' and other aspects contributing to his spaces of enunciation. Mignolo's situation is pervasively articulated in the work of contemporary diasporic South Asian intellectuals, who express, in a variety of genres, the senses in which they are never comfortably at home. Part of a large diaspora from India that began in the nineteenth century, they are a product of an enormous 'demographic dislocation' and are participants in an influential literary culture that re-inflects notions of territorial identity. As the writer, Amitav Ghosh, has put it, India itself has been re-spatialized to include a greatly extended periphery: 'India lies all over the globe.'[137]

Here, I want to emphasize a particular piece of work produced by a diasporic South Asian, Mira Nair. Her film, *The Perez Family* (1995), a story about the experience of Cuban exiles who travel to Florida as part of the last major Cuban exodus allowed by Fidel Castro, the Mariel exodus, is, at one level, a simple story of romantic reversals. Juan Perez, who has spent twenty years in prison, is finally headed for a reunion with his wife, who had emigrated twenty years earlier. Both have entertained fantasies of their reconciliation that tended to repress sensitivity to the differences that their respective twenty years of becoming might have engendered. But before the story is over, Juan falls in love with Dorita, whom he meets during his exodus, and his wife displaces her reawakened romantic feelings on a customs officer in the Miami area.

But, at another level, the film politicizes the issue of the 'homeland' and the 'family' and thereby provides an effective counter narrative to the unreflective security politics of *Father of the Bride II*, with which this analysis began. Vagaries of immigration laws and other structures of inclusion and exclusion end up constructing a 'Perez family' that is thrown together by forces beyond the control of any of the individuals. Juan and Dorita, who happen to share the surname, Perez, team up to pass successfully, as a married couple, through the first line of interrogation by immigration inspectors. They more or less adopt an eccentric and confused elderly Mr Perez while awaiting release from the Orange Bowl football stadium, an icon of US culture, where the new Mariel exodus arrivals are held. Finally, they also adopt another Perez, a young Cuban vendor, whom they meet in the process of buying his wares. Ultimately, this new Perez family, arbitrarily constituted by a combination of geo-political structures and events, becomes a family held together by bonds of caring.

Christine Bell's novel and Mira Nair's film are not the typical American family stories. If we resist the mythologizing of family life that is recycled in films like *Father of the Bride II* and look instead at the various micro narratives that contest the model of a unitary national cultural presumed in such mainstream tales, the Perez family story – a story of a family produced through a variety of structurally induced decisions – can be located in a more general frame of modernity's diasporic cultural dynamics. As a film about diaspora, directed by a director with a diasporic identity, the film is sensitive to various disjunctures: those between 'official and private memory' and those produced by the 'violent spatiotemporal disjunctions that characterize diasporan experience'.[138]

Historically, global dynamics have produced a variety of hybrid family structures. For example, there is an ethnically hybrid community in California of 'Punjabi Mexican Americans' which has its origin in a group of Punjabi men who migrated to California at the turn of the century. Because of anti-miscegenation laws, racism towards non-white peoples, and various financial hardships, they ended up marrying Mexican-American women.[139] There are various ways to frame the story, but Purnima Mankekar's version is especially apropos here. She notes that the marriage choices and subsequent elections of ethnicity by the marriages' progeny constitute a 'counter-narrative' that 'interrogates dominant histories of the United States'. This counternarrative tells us 'how diasporic subjects can (and do) forge coalitions based on a politics of location'[140] and provides the basis for a rethinking of the politics of identity and space. Mankekar enacts this rethinking by suggesting that these families constitute a situation of 'political bifocality' which 'foregrounds the ability of diasporic subjects to build alliances with struggles for social justice in *both* our homes', that is in the old homeland as well as in the place to which they have immigrated.[141]

With the making of a film version of *The Perez Family* Mira Nair forges such a complicated coalition. Her own diasporic identity is exemplary. She grew up in a small town in eastern India, graduated from Harvard, lived and worked in New York, and then moved to Kampala, were she lives with her Asian-Ugandan husband.[142] Salman Rushdie has described well the new angles of vision that derive from the experiences of such diasporic South Asians: 'We are now partly of the West. Our identity is at once plural and partial . . . If literature is in part the business of finding new angles at which to enter reality, then once again our distance, our long geographical perspective, may provide us with such angles.'[143]

Film is a special kind of literature, however. Through its various forms, it adds dimensions to the special angles of vision that a writer/director can offer. The film genre provides, for example, the possibility of resistance to official national stories, beyond what is imposed by the special vision of the diasporic director. By combining and staging encounters among different vernacular idioms and – through montage – allowing alternative cultural worlds to converge, the film can resist merely mapping the subjectivities organized by the characters' perceptions and produce what Deleuze calls time images.[144]

Throughout the film, for example, pre-revolution Cuban returns as the Mariel exodus narrative is interrupted by cuts to Juan's dreams. While at times, the use of flashbacks in films are simple devices to locate antecedent causes, in the case of Juan's dream sequences, they serve as critical time images related to both nationhood and personhood. At the level of the nation, they show that 'Cuba' is not simply a fixed territorial entity but something that exists differently in the context of different kinds of historical memory. In this sense, the flashback deepens the enigmas surrounding Cuba rather than supplying clarifying background.[145] At the level of the person, Juan's dream sequences disrupt a simplified model of individual identity by providing a non-linear glimpse of the relations within which his capacity for connecting with others is shaped.[146] Juan, like the other personae in *The Perez Family*, is always in a process of becoming, which no simple set of designations can capture.

In addition to its interruptions and temporal juxtapositions, the film genre offers 'a carnivalesque style of narrative texture'[147] which effectively mocks the official stories through which national cultures fantasize their coherence and uniformity. 'Cuba' exists as a historical, class society based on its colonized mode of capitalism: shown in Juan's dream sequences; as a contemporary pre-revolutionary society: shown in the shots of Cuban Miami, and finally as contested terrain: shown in the exchanges of hostility between the Cuban authorities and Mariel émigrés and between the conservative, bourgeois Miami Cuban community and the new Mariel arrivals, whose racial and class attributes 'disturbed Cuban Miami's collective memory'.[148]

Cuban Miami's reaction to the 'Marielitos' is represented in the extraordinary security consciousness of Juan's brother-in-law, who tries to prevent Juan's reunion with his wife by denying his identity as his brother-in-law and by fortifying his sister's home with a security alarm, special locks, and a handgun. But before the story ends, the different Cubas interact in various ways but, perhaps most notably, at a Cuban dance and music carnival.

Indeed, it was the carnivalesque nature of Christine Bell's novel version of *The Perez Family* that attracted Nair and encouraged her to see its filmic potential, especially when added to her idea, which she already had explored in *Mississippi Massala*, that the theme of 'exile and dislocation' are 'peculiarly cinematic'.[149] Added to what is intrinsic to the film genre and the potential of the story itself is of course the resonance between Nair's diasporic identity and the diaspora represented in *The Perez Family* story. As she noted:

> When I read Christine Bell's novel of *The Perez Family*, I was immediately drawn to its poetic, interior world of exile clashing directly with the brash new world of America. This was a territory that I had inhabited . . . this could be my world, these could be my people.[150]

Thus in *The Perez Family* we have the product of one historical diaspora framing the story of another, and, in the process, intervening in the politics of security that mainstream family stories (like *Father of the Bride II*) reflect. The interaction of topai – an extended India, a United States constructed of diasporic micro narratives, a Cuba extended from Cuban to Florida's 'little Havana', and historically extended as well into separate exodus waives and individual stories – shows the arbitrariness of the idea of the homeland, the family, and territorial identity.

What is impugned, moreover, is the paradigmatic, cultural enclave strategy of Huntington. The filmic articulation of a small part of the world of diaspora and the choices it enjoins locates us in a world constructed on the basis of a different, more politically perspicuous and ethically hospitable geographic imaginary, one attuned to personhood as an open-ended dynamic of becoming and to uncoded spaces within the coded space of the nation as arenas of resistance to the politics of security.

Nair's *Perez Family* enacts the possibility of an ethico-political sensitivity characteristic of what Ghosh and Sarkar have called a 'cinema of displacement', a genre produced by 'liminars', those who occupy a "slippery zone" between the two "structural force-fields" of the "home" and the "host" social systems'.[151] The insights the film encourages comport well with the ethico-political implications of the rhetoric of global space in the work of another Indian intellectual, Arjun Appadurai, especially as it intervenes in the dominant understanding of the cultural coherence of the West in general and the United States in particular.

With respect to arguments of the cultural uniqueness of western industrialized zones, Appadurai points out that the 'diasporic public spheres' one witnesses in the films of Mira Nair – for example, *Mississippi Massala*, the story of an encounter between diasporic Indians and African-Americans in Mississippi, as well as *The Perez Family* – 'are part of the cultural dynamic of urban life in most countries and continents', in which migration and mass mediation constitute a new sense of 'the globe as modern and the modern as global'.[152] As a result of such dynamics, which are no longer exceptional, the United States cannot construct itself on the basis of a cultural singularity. Accordingly, rather than as a homogeneous national culture, Appadurai figures the United States as a 'vast free trade zone' by which he means that, culturally speaking, it is a place where singularities rarely hold, where pressures towards exchange and commoditization heavily inflect both attempts at universalizing and particularizing practices and identities.[153] A hospitality to becoming is predicated on the recognition that 'trade' in this sense impeaches a politics of security.

Notes

1. Michel Serres, 'Jules Verne's Strange Journeys', *Yale French Studies*, no. 52, pp. 176–7.
2. For interviews with the writers and producers see Bruce A. Block, '*Father of the Bride* Heads Down the Aisle Again', *American Cinematographer*, 73:2 (February 1992), pp. 54–66.
3. Samuel Huntington, *The Clash of Civilizations and the Remaking of World Order* (New York: Simon and Schuster, 1996), p. 318.
4. Fredric Jameson, *The Geopolitical Aesthetic: Cinema and Space in the World System* (Bloomington: Indiana University Press, 1995), p. 10.
5. Immanuel Kant, 'Perpetual Peace', trans. H. B. Nisbet, in Hans Reiss (ed.), *Kant: Political Writings* (New York: Cambridge University Press, 1991), pp. 107–8.
6. Immanuel Kant, 'The Contest of Faculties', in Reiss (ed.), *Kant: Political Writings*, p. 181.
7. Ibid., p. 171.
8. Bernard McGrane, *Beyond Anthropology* (New York: Columbia University Press, 1989), p. 32.
9. See the translation of Kant's *Physische Geographie* by J. A. May, in J. A. May, *Kant's Concept of Geography and its Relation to recent Geographic Thought* (Toronto: University of Toronto Press, 1970), p. 255–64.
10. Walter Mignolo, *The Darker Side of the Renaissance* (Ann Arbor: University of Michigan Press, 1995), p. 10.
11. Ibid.
12. The Meso-American treatment of both history and space in their maps is treated in Gordon Brotherston, *Book of the Fourth World* (New York: Cambridge University Press, 1992).
13. Immanuel Kant, *Critique of Pure Reason*, Bk II, Ch. 3, trans. Norman Kemp Smith (London: Macmillan, 1970), p. 257.
14. Jean-François Lyotard, 'The Sign of History', trans. Geoff Bennington, in Andrew Benjamin (ed.), *The Lyotard Reader* (Cambridge, MA: Basil Blackwell, 1989), p. 398.

15. Kant, *Perpetual Peace.*
16. Avtal Brah, *Cartographies of Diaspora* (London: Routledge, 1996), p. 195.
17. See first of all, Foucault's gloss on Kant and critique in 'What is Enlightenment?' in Paul Rabinow and William M. Sullivan (eds), *Interpretive Social Science: A Second Look* (Berkeley: University of California Press, 1987), pp. 157–74, and for a more focused discussion trans. from which the quotation is drawn, see his 'What is Critique?', Lysa Hochroth, in Michel Foucault, *The Politics of Truth*, (ed.), Sylvere Lotringer and Lysa Hochroth (New York: Semiotext(e), 1997), p. 29.
18. Ibid., p. 59.
19. On this point, see William E. Connolly's 'The New Cult of Civilizational Superiority', *Theory and Event*, 2:4 (1999), http://musc.jhu.edu/journals/tae/.
20. See Kant's *Theoretical Philosophy 1755–1770*, trans. David Walford (New York: Cambridge University Press, 1992). My observations on this aspect of Kant are aided by Willi Goetschel's *Constituting Critique: Kant's Writing as Critical Praxis*, trans. Eric Schwab (Durham, NC: Duke University Press, 1994), p. 107.
21. I have treated this aspect of Kafka's writing in an analysis of his story, 'The Burrow', in Michael J. Shapiro, 'The Politics of Fear', in *Reading the Postmodern Polity* (Minneapolis: University of Minnesota Press, 1992).
22. Gilles Deleuze and Félix Guattari, *Kafka, Or Towards a Minor Literature*, trans. Dana Polan (Minneapolis: University of Minnesota press, 1986), p. 26.
23. Ibid., p. 16.
24. Gilles Deleuze and Félix Guattari, *What is Philosophy?*, trans. Hugh Tomlinson and Graham Burchell (New York: Columbia University Press, 1994), p. 58.
25. Ibid., pp. 61–83.
26. The quotations are from Donald Carter, 'The Art of the State: Difference and Other Abstractions', *Journal of Historical Sociology* 7:1 (March 1994), pp. 73–102 at p. 74.
27. Ibid. It should be added that 'Europe' was always a dubious entity. Its construction as a 'continent', which suggests natural division, is unsupportable on standard geographical as well as ethnological grounds. See Martin W. Lewis and Karen E. Wigen, *The Myth of Continents* (Berkeley: University of California Press, 1997).

28. See Arjun Appadurai, *Modernity at Large* (Minneapolis: University of Minnesota Press, 1996), pp. 10–11.
29. Edward E. Sampson, 'The Challenge of Social Change for Psychology: Globalization and Psychology's Theory of the Person', *American Psychologist*, 44:6 (June 1989), p. 917.
30. Ibid.
31. For a politically perspicuous analysis of the depoliticizing impetus of modern academic psychology, see Ellen Herman, *The Romance of American Psychology* (Berkeley: University of California Press, 1994).
32. Jacques Derrida, *Specters of Marx*, trans. Peggy Kamuf (New York: Routledge, 1994).
33. Stephen H. Collins, 'The Move to Globalization', *Journal of Accountancy*, 167 (1989), p. 82.
34. *Journal of Accountancy* (1905), p. 40.
35. Hegel, ever the advocate of the necessity of the ethical life, argued, in one of his earliest works (c. 1795), that the relationship between the commercial life and the ethical life (*Sittlichkeit*) is tragic, for from the point of view of the ethical life, the commercial life is both necessary and destructive: G. W. F. Hegel, *Natural Law*, trans. T. M. Knox (Philadelphia: University of Pennsylvania Press, 1962), pp. 94–5.
36. Ralph W. Estes, 'The Accountant's Social Responsibility', *Journal of Accountancy*, 129 (1970), p. 41.
37. This is Fredric Jameson's expression in 'Marx's Purloined Letter', *New Left Review*, 209 (1995), p. 98.
38. Joyce Oldham Appleby, *Economic Thought and Ideology in Seventeenth-Century England* (Princeton, N.J.: Princeton University Press, 1978), p. 3.
39. Ibid., pp. 52–3.
40. Ibid., p. 55.
41. Collins, 'The Move to Globalization', p. 82.
42. Ibid.
43. Georg Simmel, 'Money in Modern Culture', trans. Mark Ritter and Sam Whimster *Theory, Culture and Society*, 8 (1991), p. 17.
44. Collins, 'The Move to Globalization', p. 82.
45. Ibid., p. 83.
46. Collins, 'The Move to Globalization', p. 84. It is worth noting that in his analysis of globalization, Jacques Derrida lists ten aspects, which include various forms of disadvantage like unemployment and homelessness: Derrida, *Specters of Marx*.

47. Collins, 'The Move to Globalization', p. 84.
48. Simmel, 'Money in Modern Culture', p. 30.
49. My distinctions here are owed to the analysis in Igor Kopytoff, 'The Cultural Biography of Things: Commoditization as Process', in Arjun Appadurai (ed.), *The Social Life of Things* (New York: Cambridge University Press, 1986), pp. 64–91.
50. Ibid., p. 85.
51. Jonathan Crary, *Techniques of the Observer* (Cambridge, MA: MIT Press, 1991), p. 10.
52. See for example the discussion in Jonathan Parry and Maurice Bloch, 'Introduction', in Parry and Bloch (eds), *Money and the Morality of Exchange* (New York: Cambridge University Press, 1989), pp. 1–32.
53. Max Stackhouse, 'The Theological Challenge of Globalization', *The Christian Century*, 106 (1989), p. 470.
54. Ibid., p. 468.
55. Ibid.
56. Thomas F. O'Meara, 'Foreword', to Karl Rahner and Karl Lehmann, *Kerygma and Dogma*, trans. William Glen-Doepel (New York: Herder and Herder, 1969), p. 8.
57. Rahner and Lehmann, *Kerygma and Dogma*, pp. 15–16.
58. Stackhouse, 'The Theological Challenge of Globalization', p. 468.
59. See Bernard Lewis, *Islam and the West* (New York: Oxford University Press, 1993), p. 7.
60. Stackhouse, 'The Theological Challenge of Globalization', p. 471.
61. Peter Brown, *Authority and the Sacred* (New York: Cambridge University Press, 1995), pp. 11–12.
62. Ibid., p. 9.
63. Ibid., p. 69.
64. Lewis, *Islam and the West*, p. vii.
65. Ibid., p. 5.
66. Ibid., p. 6.
67. Ibid. While Lewis effectively identifies some important similarities between Christianity and Islam and also isolates some of the mis-recognitions historically evident in Christianity's response to Islam, he greatly overstates the extent to which Islamic states are inseparable from Islamic religious doctrine. For a more equivocal picture of the political–religious relationship in the history of Islam, see Ira M. Lapidus, 'State and

Religion in Islamic societies', *Past and Present*, 151 (1996), pp. 3–27.

68. The apology of Al Kindy in the ninth century is one of the earliest known exhortations to Muslims to embrace the (true) Christian faith. Al Kindy mounts a defence of the Christian idea of the trinity against some interpretations of Mohammed contained in the Koran and heaps abuse on the 'Coran':

> The truth, in short, is that the Coran with its manifold defects could only have appeared a miracle of eloquence and learning in the eyes of rude ignorant tribes and barbarous races.'

See Al Kindy, *The Apology of Al Kindy: Written at the Court of Al Mamun 830 AD) In Defence of Christianity Against Islam* ed. and trans. Sir William Muir (New York: E and J.B. Young and Co., 1887), 2nd edn, 81.

The modern apologetics aimed at Islam have been less vociferous but equally steadfast in their certainty about where the truth is located. Predicating Muslims' resistance to the true faith on their lack of knowledge rather than their adherence to what is 'dark and evil' the apologetic method must, as one theologian puts it, confront people belonging to organized religions with a knowledge of where and how their doctrines mislead. While all that is required to convince 'men' of 'lower culture' and 'less organized religions' is for them to see 'the Christian life in action', one must confront 'obstacles of the mind', and obstacles of the 'hard heart and wayward will' as well in the case of organized religions like Islam. See Lawrence E. Browne, *The Quickening Word: A Theological Answer to the Challenge of Islam* (Cambridge: W. Heffer and Sons, 1955), p. 5. The writer's heightened respect for such 'organized religions' as Islam leads him to study Islamic doctrine with care and to urge, as a result, that Christian doctrine be clearly presented, particularly in cases in which its truths contradict the teachings of Islam.

69. Stackhouse, 'The Theological Challenge of Globalization', p. 470.
70. Ibid.
71. Ibid., p. 471.
72. Dennis M. Campbell, 'Why Should Anyone Believe? Apologetics and Theological Education', *The Christian Century*, 106 (1989), p. 136.
73. Ibid., p. 138.

74. Michel Foucault, 'Governmentality' in Graham Burchell, Colin Gordon, and Peter Miller (eds), *The Foucault Effect* (Chicago: University of Chicago Press, 1991), pp. 87–8.

75. In his analysis of the vagaries of that historical performance, Vassilis Lambroupoulus has approvingly quoted the hyperbolic remark of a literary scholar: 'For nearly two millennia, Christianity has been little other than a critical enterprise', in *The Rise of Eurocentrism* (Princeton, N.J.: Princeton University Press, 1993), p. 237.

76. For a gloss on Paul's interpretive practices, see Daniel Boyarin, *A Radical Jew: Paul and the Politics of Identity* (Berkeley: University of California Press, 1994).

77. See Samuel Huntington, 'The Clash of Civilizations', *Foreign Affairs*, 72 (1993), pp. 27–43, and *The Clash of Civilizations and the Remaking of World Order*.

78. See Fredric Jameson, *The Geopolitical Aesthetic: Cinema and Space in the World System* (Bloomington, Indiana University Press, 1992), p. 4.

79. Michael Taussig, *The Nervous System* (New York: Routledge, 1992), p. 115.

80. Bradley Klein, *Strategic Studies and World Order* (Cambridge: Cambridge University Press, 1994), p. 20.

81. On this point, see Michael Dillon, *Politics of Security* (New York: Routledge, 1996).

82. Jens Bartelson, *A Genealogy of Sovereignty* (New York: Cambridge University Press, 1995), p. 165.

83. Ibid.

84. Ibid., p. 213.

85. Ibid.

86. On this historical practice, see Edward A. Tiryakian, 'Three Metacultures of Modernity', *Theory, Culture and Society*, 13 (1996), pp. 99–118.

87. These features of globalization are emphasized by Mary Louise Pratt', Comparative Literature and Global Citizenship', in Charles Bernheimer (ed.), *Comparative Literature in the Age of Multiculturalism* (Baltimore: Johns Hopkins University Press, 1995), p. 59.

88. Huntington, *The Clash of Civilizations*, p. 30.

89. The issue of the 'violence of representation' is treated in Jacques Derrida's reading of the thought of Emmanuel Levinas: 'Violence and Metaphysics', in *Writing and Difference*,

trans. Alan Bass (Chicago: University of Chicago Press, 1978), pp. 79–153.

90. Joseph Conrad, 'Geography and Some Explorers', in *Last Essays* (New York: Doubleday, Page and Co, 1926), pp. 1–21.
91. On this point, see the discussion in J. B. Harley, 'Cartographic Ethics and Social Theory', *Cartographica*, 27 (1990), pp. 1–23.
92. Claude Nicolet, *Space, Geography, and Politics in the Early Roman Empire* (Ann Arbor: University of Michigan Press, 1991), p. 5.
93. Ibid., p. 8.
94. The perspective and quotations here are from Richard Helgerson, 'The Land Speaks: Cartography, Chorography, and Subversion in Renaissance England', *Representations*, 16: 4 (Fall 1986), p. 56. It was also the case, more generally in England that, by the end of the sixteenth century, the process of consolidating the state form was accompanied by 'an unprecedented explosion in the making of maps'. See Philip Corrigan and Derek Sayer, *The Great Arch* (Oxford: Basil Blackwell, 1985), p. 70.
95. Helgerson, 'The Land Speaks', p. 62.
96. Shawn Irlam, 'Gerrymandered Geographies: Exoticism in Thomson and Chateaubriand', *MLN*, 108:5 (December 1993), p. 892.
97. Ibid.
98. Huntington, *The Clash of Civilizations*, p. 36.
99. See Lapidus, 'State and Religion in Islamic societies'.
100. Huntington, *The Clash of Civilizations*, p. 116.
101. This expression is Foucault's in 'Governmentality'.
102. Peter J. Taylor, 'Beyond Containers: internationality, interstateness, interterritoriality', *Progress in Human Geography*, 19:1 (March 1995), p. 6.
103. Foucault, 'Governmentality', p. 100.
104. For this history see George Mosse, *Nationalism and Sexuality* (New York: Howard Fertig, 1985).
105. William Bennett and C. Deloris Tucker, 'Smut-Free Stores', *New York Times*, 9 December 1996, p. A15.
106. Ibid.
107. Joseph Gusfield, *The Culture of Public Problems* (Chicago: University of Chicago Press, 1981).
108. Norbert Elias, *The Civilizing Process* (Cambridge, MA: Basil Blackwell, 1994), pp. 22–4.
109. George Mosse, *Nationalism and Sexuality* (Madison, WI: University of Wisconsin Press, 1985).

110. Paul Passavant, 'The Governmentality of Discussion' (unpublished manuscript), (1997) p. 28.
111. Ibid.
112. Brian Wallis, 'Selling Nations: International Exhibitions and Cultural Diplomacy', in Daniel J. Sherman and Irit Rogoff (eds), *Museum Culture* (London: Routledge, 1994), p. 266.
113. Étienne Balibar, 'Racism and Nationalism', trans. Chris Turner in Étienne Balibar and Emmanuel Wallerstein, *Race, Nation, Class: Ambiguous Identities* (New York: Verso, 1991), p. 49.
114. Ibid., p. 57.
115. See for example, Jonathan Friedman, 'Narcissism, Roots, and Postmodernity', in *Modernity and Identity*, Scott Lash and Jonathan Friedman (eds) (Cambridge, MA: Blackwell, 1992), pp. 331–66.
116. See *Ibid.*, p. 337.
117. On this duplicity, see for example, Wade Graham, 'Masters of the Game', *Harpers*, (July 1996).
118. See for example, the symposium in *Asian Studies*, 18:1 (July 1994).
119. The expression is in Boaventura de Sousa Santos, *Toward a New Common Sense* (New York: Routledge, 1995), p. 485.
120. C. R. Whittaker, *Frontiers of the Roman Empire* (Baltimore: Johns Hopkins University Press, 1994), p. 11.
121. See Whittaker's treatment of Edward Luttwak's misreading of ancient geography Ibid., p. 6.
122. On this point, see David Campbell, 'Political Prosaics, Transversal Politics, and the Anarchical World', in Michael J. Shapiro and Hayward Alker (eds), *Challenging Boundaries* (Minneapolis: University of Minnesota Press, 1996), pp. 7–31.
123. Huntington, *The Clash of Civilizations*, p. 212.
124. This anti-essentialist gloss, which summons the resistance of time, relies on Gilles Deleuze's distinctions between space and time, where differences in degree, a spatial set of separations, allows for the 'common sense' involved in identity thinking space and differences in kind, based on temporality, defy attempts to essentialize identity. See Gilles Deleuze, *Difference and Repetition*, trans. Paul Patton (New York: Columbia University Press, 1994).
125. Huntington, *The Clash of Civilizations*, p. 30.
126. Again, the model of non-dogmatic thought is inspired by

Deleuze, who sees this kind of thought as encounter rather than representation and recognition: *Difference and Repetition*, p. 139.

127. Jacques Derrida, *The Other Heading*, p. 6.

128. Ibid., pp. 19–20.

129. Kant imagined that only 'European' nations had a distinctive national character and the ability to become self-reflective in encounters with others. See *Anthropology from a Pragmatic Point of View*, pp. 225–36.

130. Ibid., p. 7.

131. Ibid., p. 30.

132. This is Richard Beardsworth's apt characterization of Derrida's political agenda in *Derrida and the Political* (New York Routledge, 1996).

133. Jacques Derrida, 'Onto-Theology of National-Humanism (Prolegomena to a Hypothesis)', *Oxford Literary Review*, 14:1 (1992), p. 17.

134. This is not to suggest that all diasporic intellectuals embrace progressive agendas. For an argument against overdrawing the assumption that they do, see Katharyne Mitchell, 'Different Diasporas and the Hype of Hybridity', *Society and Space*, 15:5 (October 1997), pp. 533–53,

135. Walter D. Mignolo, *The Darker Side of the Renaissance*: *Literacy, Territoriality, and Colonization* (Ann Arbor: University of Michigan Press, 1995), p. 6.

136. Ibid., p. 15.

137. Amitav Ghosh, 'The Diaspora in Indian Culture', *Public Culture*, 2:1 (Fall 1989), p. 78.

138. The quotations are from Laura U. Marks, 'A Deleuzian Politics of Hybrid Cinema', *Screen*, 35:2 (Autumn 1994), p. 245. In addition to explicating Deleuze's political insights in his cinema analyses, Marks reviews the special insights of what she calls 'experimental diasporan cinema'.

139. See Karen Isaksen Leonard, *Making Ethnic Choices*: *California's Punjabi Mexican Americans* (Philadelphia: Temple University Press, 1992).

140. Purnima Mankekar, 'Reflections on Diasporic Identities: A Prolegomenon to an Analysis of Political Bifocality', *Diaspora*, 3:3 (Winter 1994), p. 350.

141. Ibid., p. 368.

142. This short biographical note is paraphrased from an interview.

See Peggy Orenstein, 'Salaam America!: An Interview with Mira Nair', *Mother Jones* (January/February 1992), pp. 60–1.

143. Salman Rushdie, *Imaginary Homelands* (New York: Viking, 1991), p. 15.

144. In *Cinema 1*, Deleuze identifies the subjective image in which the perspective of a person who is part of a set of interactions governs their meanings (p. 71), whereas with time images, which Deleuze elaborates in *Cinema 2*, the composition of shots constructs a commentary that resists both official and subjective perspectives.

145. See Deleuze, *Cinema 2*, p 50, for a treatment of flashbacks upon which my analysis here is based.

146. Deleuze (Ibid., p. 53) refers to how flashbacks counter linear models of personhood by constituting a 'forking of time'.

147. The quotation as well as the ideas about film in these remarks are from Robert Burgoyne, 'Modernism and the Narrative of the nation in *JFK*', in Vivian Sobchack (ed.), *The Persistence of History: Cinema, Television, and the Modern Event* (New York: Routledge, 1996), p. 123.

148. Roman de la Campos, 'The Latino Diaspora in the United States: Sojourns from a Cuban Past', *Public Culture* 6 (1994), p. 296.

149. See Mira Nair's remarks on the film in 'Director's Notes', (http:www.movienet/movienet/movinfo/perezfamilynotes-dir.html).

150. Nair, 'Director's Notes'.

151. Bishnupriya Ghosh and Bhaskar Sarkar, 'The Cinema of Displacement: Towards a Politically motivated Poetics', *Film Criticism*, 20:1–2 (Fall/winter 1995–6), p. 104. The Internal quotations and the concept of the liminar are from the work of Victor Turner. See also Hamid Naficy, *The Making of Exile Cultures: Iranian Television in Los Angeles* (Minneapolis: University of Minnesota Press, 1993).

152. Appadurai, *Modernity at Large*, p. 10.

153. Ibid., pp. 42–3.

4

Value Eruptions and Modalities: The Politics of Masculinity

Introduction: An Eruption of Value Discourse

There are politically pregnant moments in which different domains of cultural expression are interarticulated to unite seemingly disparate linguistic domains. Episodes of metaphoric slippage – for example the expression of anxiety about gender or sexual ambiguity in a discourse used to distinguish genuine from false money – reveal a complex imbrication of cultural-meaning practices and provide insight into how valuing practices emerge and become politicized. Such episodes are aspects of what Jean-Luc Nancy calls 'finite history': history in the sense of a series of events in which people share a time without natural boundaries and relationships without definite warrants such as 'nature' or 'reason'.[1] Because the occasions of metaphorical transfer lack stable foundations, they are finite historical events that show how valuing is a historically situated and politically charged cultural practice, inseparable from its modalities of expression.

This analysis begins with one such event, reported in connection with an anthropological investigation. In an account of her ethnographic work in Indian villages, Susan Seizer, an anthropologist with a same-sex partner, describes a situation in which she and her partner's lesbian identities risked disintegration in a place that had no language or social position for women with female partners. The story takes various twists and turns as Seizer and her partner, Kate, seek to establish a modus vivendi that will allow their relationship to survive while allowing Seizer to retain the rapport necessary to accomplish her field work. They ultimately live much of the time in separate cities.

On one of the infrequent occasions in which they manage to live together – they are house-sitting for a bourgeois family in a major city – they find they have difficulty having sex in the 'master bedroom', because Angela, a house servant, is not respectful of their desire for privacy. The heterosexual intimacy of the master bedroom makes sense to Angela, and under normal circumstances, while her master and mistress are at home, she stays off the second floor. But her deferential attitude towards heterosexual union does not carry over to a lesbian relationship. Accordingly, when she became privy to a 'primal scene' – she witnessed the two women making love – and had no words (in Tamil) for lesbian sexuality, she represented the sexual activity (through a mediating interpreter) as 'minting money'. In short, lesbians, for Angela, are counterfeiters. Although for Angela, this means that the relationship is illicit, Seizer found the translation both gratifying and horrifying. At least her relationship was finally being figured locally in terms of value.

Angela had it right in a way, she and her partner Kate were valuable to each other: 'She gave us the translation into local currency that we'd been looking for, horrifying as it was.'[2] And, more generally, Seizer recognized the powerful undercurrents that the translation revealed:

> The complicated web of discursive experiential and subjective association that allowed Angela to see counterfeiting, and not sex, value and not affect, money and not intimacy when she flung open the bedroom door one fine summer morning surely indicates a sex-money-power nexus that contains rich deposits for future study and a veritable gold mine for metaphor theory.[3]

To treat this episode critically, we must recognize, as I have suggested, that the issue of metaphor is inseparable from questions of value. Contrary to the still prevalent, Aristotelian, view that metaphor rests on resemblance, is the inquiry-enabling view, inspired by Nietzsche, that productions of metaphoric equivalence constitute valuing practices.[4] To inquire into such productions is to disclose a power–knowledge–value circuit; it is to discern the operations of power and authority in the discourses that lend value to the boundaries practices constituting personhood. Two aspects of Angela's response are compelling for purposes of inquiry. First is the event itself: the eruption of a discourse on value in response to what she saw; and second is the modality of that discourse: that the expression of value should take the metaphorical turn that it did, connecting lesbian sex with counterfeiting. These two registers of value, the 'when' and the 'how' of value, contrast with the more familiar mode of value questioning which seeks to clarify 'what' values are.

In contrast with a focus on the temporality of value's emergence and the modality of value's expression is a neo-Kantian tradition that seeks to gain 'knowledge' of values, where values are referents that emerge from shared structures of apprehension and knowledge is based on a structure of representation thought to be reflective of a common sense with a universalizing trajectory. Although Kantian philosophy provided a frame for resisting a simplistic, representational approach to value, attentive as it was to specific historical events and their subsequent polemical influences, mainstream neo-Kantian approaches fail to share Kant's ambivalence about representation and treat values as referents rather than events. In a review of John Gray's intellectual biography of Sir Isaiah Berlin, for example, Alan Ryan reproduces this objectifying model by addressing the issue of whether one can publicly reason about primary values as opposed to instrumental ones. Referring to Berlin's (and Gray's) affirmation that there are no unitary 'ends of life', Ryan notes that 'there is no right answer to the question of which life is the best one for us, individually or generally'.[5] This construction of the issue is only possible within a representational model, in which one raises the question of *what* is a value: that is, the epistemologically oriented question of the thingness of a value.[6]

Ryan's remarks on Berlin, Gray, and liberal discourse provide a further contrast between objectifying and non-representational analytics; he describes Gray's 'agonistic liberalism' as 'the thought that a free society is a place where individuals and indeed the whole society work out their own particular fates'.[7] While Ryan's sentiments here make no explicit reference to valuing, they reproduce a particular historical practice of liberalism. Ryan articulates a discourse on the social order that contains a normative problematic constructing the 'individual' and the separation between individual and society.

Such implicit valuing commitments raise questions worthy of inquiry. They should be treated as symptoms, as Nietzsche noted, not as calls to make simple judgements, for or against.[8] Accordingly, if we take a genealogical view and resist being drawn into the problematic controlled by the liberal discourse on the singularity of personhood, we are able to recognize that the ordinary individual emerged as a describable personage in various writing genres (like biography) in the eighteenth century as part of a more general development that Foucault has called 'procedure[s] of objectification'.[9] Insofar as valuing makes an appearance in this emergence, it is immanent in the discursive production of the referents. Rather than asking about the value of such discursive objects as 'the individual', a question that allows the valuing involved in the production of the referents to remain unaddressed and therefore non-contentious, one can frame questions about how value is in evidence in the emergence of the referents. Such a perspective requires what Foucault called 'patience'.[10] It requires inquiry into the conditions of emergence of such historical subjects as the 'individual'.

If we reject representational thinking and recognize instead that valuing – in both academic and everyday life – is a radically contingent, spatio-temporally delimited practice, not a process of discovering stable features of either the world (the position of empiricists and naturalists) or the representational structures of subjects (the Kantian model), we can engage in inquiry into how 'value' arises from historically situated human actions, articulations, and involvements. Nevertheless, Kant sets the tone for this analysis; he recognized that 'things' are present to human subjects only insofar as value is imposed as part of the way they *produce* their worlds. But resisting Kant's restriction of that production to a narrative of understanding: to a production that takes place within mental life, reflecting only the activity of faculties, we can locate that productivity in the practices and technologies by which difference is distinguished and persons are oriented to the life-world in connection with various pro-jects.

This analysis is focused on a particular project, the work of constituting masculinity, a normative model of personhood that is located in the interface between practices of the self and processes of social identification. It requires attention to the way that the value of male identity is implicated in a variety of forms of cultural expression and is aimed at disclosing the value issues circulating around some contemporary defences of traditional, normative masculinity. More specifically, inspired by Angela's contribution to a value event, I assemble a conceptual and historical montage to encourage critical thinking about the co-occurrence of two cultural anxieties: fears that give rise to defences of the identity boundaries of gender and sexuality and the articulation of those fears with concerns about the value of representational forms of money.

Rampaging White Men

In various genres of cultural expression in the USA in the 1980s, normative masculinity was in focus. For example, white male heroes in some Hollywood feature films were on a rampage, reasserting a form of maleness perceived to be threatened with extinction. It was a time in which popular culture had become a battle ground. Models of personhood were in contention to be the masculine avatar of a potent nationhood.[11] While the male body was the primary site of contestation, the contention had allegorical significance for the character of the nation. The male heroes, the Rambos, Robocops et al., pitted themselves not only against threats to America's moral coherence within and without but also against bureaucrats and political leaders, who were represented as either corrupt and self-serving or overly intrusive in the lives of good citizens.

As Susan Jeffords has noted, these 'hard body' heroes articulated well with the Reagan presidency, which represented itself as an effort both to remasculinize the nation after what was widely perceived as a global post-Vietnam impotence and a feminized presidency during the Carter years and to get government off the backs of the average citizen.[12] The masculinity agonism has continued. In the 1990s, 'white men' off-screen have continued the rampage within their home venues. For example, in his ethnography of men's solidarity and militia movements, conducted while on an excursion to his home town, Fred Pfeil disclosed an issue that has continually reasserted itself in the struggles though which men have, historically, sought to achieve and protect various versions of a masculine self. Both movements, one oriented towards recovering a tradition of wisdom, and the other towards *ressentiment*, are 'characterized', he notes, 'by widespread confusion as to what men, including perhaps white men, are *supposed* to be, mean, and do, and a related uncertainty about the United States – as a polity certainly, but even more as what Benedict Anderson calls an "imagined community" is about'.[13]

Pfeil's former community offers an exemplary expression of a more general cultural anxiety, focused on an increasingly problematic personhood and its connections with images of nationhood. These anxieties and the movements they have spawned have been annexed by political campaigns at both state and national levels. Those seeking to collect grievances do so by positioning themselves against government's tolerance of cultural diversity, against the globalization of domestic economy, against women's control over their bodies and a share of civic space, against welfare and other entitlements, against affirmative action, against extending rights to gays and lesbians, and against open immigration policy and official tolerance of 'illegal aliens'. But beyond the particular objects of resentment, the modalities of expression of anxiety and anger are connected to a more general project of identity maintenance.

The kind of interarticulations evident in the contemporary

expressions of anger and concern have surfaced in earlier periods. A cut to a scene in the eighteenth century, involving a 'problematic collision (and collusion) between the commodification of woman and the idealization of chastity',[14] for example, provides a propitious venue for an initial, edifying leap into the past; it supplies a time image that yields a critical focus on the present. It was a commonplace in various eighteenth-century texts for the language of commercial fraud to be applied to cases in which a sexually experienced woman attempted to pass herself off as virginal:

> Counterfeit virginity appears in guides to the sights of London, in poems about bawds and prostitutes, in such novels as John Cleland's *Fanny Hill, or Memoirs of a Woman of Pleasure* (1748–49), Daniel Defoe's *Moll Flanders* (1722), and Tobias Smollett's *The Adventures of Roderick Random* (1748), and in popular home guides to matters of reproduction.[15]

There is a significant historical context for this textual preoccupation. The writing occurs in a period in which the understanding of the female body was undergoing a marked conceptual alteration. During the eighteenth century a change in models of sexual difference – from one sex and two genders to two sexes – was taking place. While the change, registered most unambiguously in medical texts, involved an epistemological shift – a revised version of female anatomy[16] – its implications in cultural texts were more ontological and social. The altered view of anatomy implicated notions of attraction between sexual opposites, and the resulting change in sensibilities was reflected in other genres. Among other things, there developed a keen interest in illicit sex and a corresponding concern with fraudulent virginity. Because sexuality had become more commodified, and virginity had, accordingly, become an object of consumption rather than just a cultural value, the question of the counterfeit 'maidenhead' became a prominent theme.[17] And, most significantly for purposes here, the theme linked a concern with genuine versus counterfeit currency with virginity as a sexual currency that could be debased without detection. Depending on one's gender position with respect to proof of virginity – realized in either its detection or disguising – the evidence that virginity 'is not ultimately verifiable through the body' was either 'disturbing or enabling'.[18]

What was enabling for some women was disturbing for some men. To appreciate the disturbance is to recognize the ways in which a male-dominated social order was reacting to a knowledge problem that rendered the value of woman-as-object unstable. That various cultural texts should frame the issue on the basis of a discourse about genuine versus false money is not surprising. Questions of value cannot be raised without substituting one set of signs for another; 'it is always through replacement that values are created'.[19] And by the eighteenth century, the money form was dominant as both a measure and exemplar of value.

However, apart from the constitutive requirement for the necessity of interarticulation in the emergence of a value problematic, understanding the emergence of value requires inquiry into why, at particular times and in particular ways, value episodes erupt and become politicized. These questions bring us back to the present historical context in which we witness expressions of identity contention raised by some white males in the USA, in particular, their attraction to anti-immigrant and anti-gay and lesbian policy initiatives. An understanding of the appeal of such initiatives requires an appreciation of some men's recently intensified concern with identity maintenance. The anti-immigrant and anti-gay and lesbian appeals strike them at a time in which there are exacerbations surrounding their performances of self. While there is a wide range of responses to altered performance demands, here I am focusing on the more extravagant examples.

To appreciate the rage and anxiety that is being exploited by various political movements, it is necessary to appreciate the energy that goes into identity maintenance. Certainly there are abundant signs that white male anxiety and rage are present. They are deployed not only on various Others – women's movements, gays, immigrants, and 'people of colour' – but also on governmental authority at various levels. With respect to the disturbance over other identities, it is evident that insofar as identity is always a continuing performance,[20] the performance demands on the white male have been heightened by significant alterations in modernity's identity economy. Whiteness and maleness can no longer claim to be zero points in the public, interpretive registers of social and cultural difference. Rather than normality, whiteness and maleness are increasingly seen as a set of problematic practices. Instead of constituting a standard against which various others can be constructed as social problems, white males are under critical observation. They are no longer merely a non-situated focal point or what Emerson called a 'transparent eye' able to surveil the world without the pressure of reciprocal scrutiny.[21]

Intensifying the displacement of the white male from the space of unquestioned normality is what Pfeil discerns as a perceived deficit. As cultural awareness heightens for various social groups, white males become a 'tribe without traditions', a group with no historical basis for coherence: 'what seems salient is the assumption that women, African-Americans, Native Americans and other non-white or non-male Others are, each and all, self-enclosed communities of people whose identities are first and foremost culturally given rather than politically and historically made'.[22]

If we locate the issues within the practices of identity maintenance and the related evocations of cultural security, it is possible to recognize the social perceptions that this intensification of identity scrutiny engenders, as white males, in particular those with relatively few resources for attracting positive recognition, strive for self-recognition within the domestic ethno- gender- and intimacy-scapes that appear to be increasingly less anchored in traditional norms. But in addition there is a need to treat with greater depth the other dimension of anxieties and hostilities that Pfeil's excursion disclosed: the migration of the confusion from the level of intergroup relations to that of a person's relation to the United States as a collective entity. One needs, in short, to treat the symbolic interactions between personhood and nationhood to examine the recent deepening hostility towards government.

Although much of the anti-government rhetoric cites specific instances of oppression form various agencies – the Internal Revenue Service, the FBI, the Bureau of Alcohol, Tobacco and Firearms – there are complex symbolic exchanges between government and 'Others' as objects of rage. Government is not merely seen as oppressive; it is also seen as warranting undeserving social identities, thereby producing an unacceptable alloy in the model of nationhood. Certainly the interrelations between models of manhood and nationhood were evoked throughout the Reagan and Bush presidencies, during which there were attempts to restore an aggressive masculinity to the American polity in the face of the perceived challenge to the United States' potency in the Vietnam War. Various analysts have established connections between the disparagement of gays and the valorization of a masculinized US presence in the world of states. This obsession with masculinity is powerfully reflected in the policing of sexualities apparent in the United States' most militarized venues, which have sought to exclude women and non-heterosexuals from the armed services and the academies from which their officer ranks are drawn.

Just as other nations are the 'Others' against whom national cohesion is to be achieved. Women are the Others against whom a coherent masculinity is to be achieved. The abjection of women (and feminine identity in general) or homosexuality (seen as feminized masculinity) as integral to the constitution of the masculine self is part of a pervasive social logic governing the valuing of identity. By seeing 'value' as not simply referential, as the relationship of a value commitment to an object, but as a frenzied 'interplay between dominance and exorbitance',[23] that is, as part of the practice of securing models of selfhood by expelling certain Others beyond approved identity boundaries, it becomes possible to see how the practice of masculine identity reacts to its paradoxical situation; it both depends on others and abjures its dependancy. Among other things, unable to accept the radical contingency of his identity, the anxious and enraged white male becomes hostile or violent.

Accordingly, the rampages represented in contemporary Hollywood films constitute a 'wresting of autonomy from an other, a vanquishing of danger implicit in the Other – in short, the willful expenditure of the Other in an imposing production of the self'.[24] It is nothing less than an extravagant rejection of one's contingency. In addition, because the Other is constitutively close to the self, the identity valuing practice of imposing a pure, non-contingent identity on the self, articulates itself as a spatial project, as acts of vigorous boundary policing. Indeed, in a variety of venues, military and otherwise, the maintenance of maleness involves a strenuous policing in which the actively homosocial, which verges on the homosexual, is not allowed to cross the boundary into the explicitly homosexual. As Susan Faludi discovered in her ethnography of a military academy, the Citadel, the retreat to an enclosed, masculine space allows a feminized intimacy to prevail without risking ascriptions of the loss of heterosexual masculinity.[25]

William Friedkin's film *To Live and Die in LA* (1985) explores this policing of the homosocial–homosexual boundary. It is the 'police', a group of detectives in pursuit of a counterfeiter, who engage in active homosocial male-bonding rituals, which include a continual use of phallic imagery and a preoccupation with showing that one has 'balls'. At the same time, it is the police who maintain rigidly heterosexual personae, while the object of their investigation, an artist/counterfeiter, has a relationship with a bisexual and androgynous-appearing woman and moves about in venues that are ambiguously gender-coded.

The policing of counterfeit money therefore functions, among other things, as a metaphor throughout the film for the policing of masculinity. To maintain the charade of an undiluted masculinity and an unambiguous sexuality, the 'police' protect the boundary between the homosocial and homosexual jealously. Eve Sedgwick, who has investigated the expression of such policing projects in the domain of English literature, has characterized this project succinctly. She notes that among men, there is a strong desire to make sure that 'the diacritical opposition between the 'homosocial' and the 'homosexual'' . . . remain 'thoroughly dichotomous'.[26] To Live and Die in LA is worthy of further scrutiny, for it incorporates much of the conceptual terrain under analysis here and provides a mode of cinematic thought that displaces the dominant structures for recognizing gender and sexuality. However to have an adequate context for the film's politicized treatment of the personhood–nationhood nexus, we need a more general and historically sensitive model of that connection.

States and Bodies

How does the authority of the state figure within the identity economy of the anxious and resentful white male? If we pursue the figure of the counterfeit, we have a conceptual vehicle to treat the way that identity practices involve the overwrought management of identity boundaries. Before money developed its dominance as the 'general equivalent' within which value discourses were structured, more material models of wealth were the primary frames within which identity warrants were elaborated. Changes in the frames would therefore necessarily produce disturbances in practices of self-recognition. To state the issue generally, the self is not only a body but also a series of material and non-material extensions. Some extensions of the self are seen as felicitous or empowering. For example, the idea of property articulated within Lockean liberalism, and juridically institutionalized as various forms of ownership, reflects a welcomed extension of the self into a material domain of concrete self-representation. Aside from being a mode for producing the investments that engender wealth, landed property has a decidedly ontological significance. Howard Horowitz has described it well:

> Property is a self-investment, the attempt to make the inalienable manifest in the forms that represent it; and thus the self-investment in property is also a self-production, for self is unavailable and unformed except in its representation through property.[27]

It should be noted, however, that this felicitous extension has an extended fiduciary aspect. 'Property' is juridical as well as material; there must be an authoritative, that is, governmental, warrant for this extension of the self. Self-reflection with respect to such a spatial extension must necessarily also involve a dependence on the warranting power of the state.[28] It is not surprising, therefore, that interpersonal and intergroup antagonisms often involve resentments over the differential warranting lent by governmental authority. These antagonisms are exacerbated during periods in which the boundaries of the self from the personal, bodily space to juridical space (new eligibilities) or media space (new forms of presence) are altered. One of these periods is associated with a crisis of masculinity at the turn of the twentieth century. As was noted in Chapter 2, the mechanical extensions lent to the working body during the development of the industrial age gave rise to concern about the depletion of masculinity because of the ambiguities attached to the agency of extended bodies.[29]

The contemporary, information age has also produced confusions related to bodily extension. As A. R. Stone has noted, agency is always grounded in physical presences – a process she calls warranting – but in the virtual age, warranting is more problematic and 'Government's response to the fragmentation of their subjects is to develop a hypertrophy of location technologies.' People are assembled and extended as fiduciary subjects by creating a paper trail of 'social security numbers, passports and street addresses' that reference each particular physical body.[30] As the trail becomes increasingly elaborate, circuitous, and out of the individual's control, hostility to the sources of its production and centres of surveillance increases. The issue here turns on how the problem of the counterfeit has become articulated within politicized episodes of identity struggle.

The Counterfeiters

The issue of counterfeiting evokes two different dimensions of policing. Counterfeiting is both a threat to money's exchange value and to its ontological value. Exchange has always served an ontological as well as a utilitarian function. As Georg Simmel noted, systems of barter were part of a series of intersubjective relationships through which persons bonded with their communities. But the 'interdependence of personality and material relationships, which is typical of the barter economy, is dissolved by the money economy'.[31] Not surprisingly therefore, people attach some of their ontological anxieties to a concern with finding a firm warrant for the value of money, not only to protect their wealth but also to reconnect their exchanges to a foundation with collective symbolic guarantees. As a result, fear of the counterfeit has significant ontological depth; it produces not only crises associated with changes in the backing of money (gold, silver, or otherwise) but also crises of meaning because of the way monetary discourses are implicated in various other domains of identity: for example, gender/sexuality.

André Gide's *The Counterfeiters* provides a useful critical review and elaboration of a crisis that involves all the relevant registers treated in the analysis thus far.[32] Among other things, the novel reflects a period of cultural anxiety; it was written during a period of crisis in realist painting and novelistic fiction, as the guarantees connecting signs and objects became unstable.[33] In addition, *The Counterfeiters* was written precisely at the time (during World War I) that France was issuing paper money no longer backed by gold. This move towards a representation of value without a material foundation provoked strong ambivalence. As Jean-Joseph Goux has noted, the novel 'expresses the contradiction between a persistent nostalgic attachment to gold currency, and a realistic, or rather theoretical acceptance of the dizzying novelty of inconvertability'.[34]

Goux suggests as well that this monetary vertigo was accompanied by a more general anxiety about the way in which social life was being appropriated by economic life, 'a collapse of certain profound ideological mediations between economic life and life proper'.[35] Moreover, Gide's novel adds a dimension of linguisticality to those of real versus false money, authentic versus inauthentic patrimonies, and genuine versus confused desires. The novel abounds with ambiguous interconnections between systems of exchange and the problem of language. A major character, Edouard, is a novelist who constantly has issues of exchange seem to usurp the roles of his characters, disturbing attempts to give their personalities a fixity.

The novel as a whole therefore forces us to conceive at once anxieties about counterfeit money and a number of other issues surrounding questions of the authenticity of registers of value. For example at the outset, a father, who is a magistrate, turns out to be a false father, and, not coincidently, his name is Profitdieu, making a religious icon an object connected to profit. And the falseness of the father seems to be mapped on to the issue of the falseness of literature, for the novel reflects the period's crisis over the realism of representation. Reflecting a variety of concerns about authentic versus inauthentic modes of representation – in language, literature, money, and sexuality – an exchange of real and counterfeit coins takes place at the centre of the story. The story as a whole obeys 'a monetary logic', as Goux points out,[36] but this logic operates within a number of different registers.

What unites these different registers is a more general crisis. Gide's *The Counterfeiters* treats a period in which value foundations are unstable, and government, which is supposed to supply the backing for value – the value of identities, of money, of public language – has lost or abdicated its position of control over warranting to a banking apparatus. Thus, in addition to operating in various 'ontological registers',[37] as it elaborates a historical crisis over which equivalents of value are to be established, the novel foregrounds anxiety about the role of the state, which has failed its fiduciary role of providing warrants for 'real' value.

Contemporary expressions of anxiety are similar inasmuch as the US government is now seen by many as having lost its control over warranting national identity because it has abdicated its control over money. However, the structures indicted are different; instead of a banking apparatus, the usurpers vary from the more proximate Federal Reserve (a favourite target of right-wing anti-government militia movements),[38] to the more distant 'New World Order' controlled, according to the influential Christian leader/writer, Pat Robertson, by a supercomputer in Brussels that handles worldwide bank clearings.[39]

But Gide's novel treats as well the interarticulations between issues of monetary currency and sexuality, and both are connected to a crisis in the authority of the state. As is the case with money, sexuality operates within the registers of true and false in Gide's novel; the love relationship between the characters Bernard and Laura, for example, is mediated and confused by the deceptions built into their statements. Moreover, Bernard's attempts to locate himself both with respect to paternity (he has a false father, the magistrate whom he learns is a stepfather) and his amorous interests (his relationship with Laura) recognize a disturbance in his affective relationship to the *state*. He explicitly affirms that 'the state is nothing but a convention' so that he need not take on feelings of inauthenticity derived from his vain attempts hitherto to give it a firm foundation or reality.[40]

William Friedkin's *To Live and Die in LA* (hereafter *LA*) operates on all the ontological registers evoked in Gide's novel. However, the historical crisis of the mid-1980s is the above- mentioned Reagan-era obsession with reasserting a heroic and unalloyed masculinity. And, rather than sublime and confused expressions of love, the amorous exchanges are more bodily than linguistic, evoked in scenes of sexual rather than epistolary and dialogic intercourse. Nevertheless, the representations attending sexual intercourse are significant parts of the story, and the linguistic register is also central to the story's meditation on the authenticity versus inauthenticity of identity. Most significantly, the modalities evinced in *LA* continue to inform the masculinity agonistics of the 1990s. Our literary/historical montage therefore cuts from interwar Paris to the Los Angeles of the 1980s.

Los Angeles in the mid-1980s

Several polarities animate the structure of William Friedkin's *LA*. At a simple narrative level, Richard Chance, a police detective, is in pursuit of Erik Masters, a counterfeiter. The chase has a lot of similarity with other eighties male rampage films, for Masters has murdered Chance's former partner. Revenge and rectification as well as controlling false currency fuels the pursuit. In addition to the cop versus criminal dimension, *LA* bears a striking similarity with other 'buddy' films. Having lost his partner, Jimmie Hart, who is murdered during his last assignment, much of the story involves the socialization of the inexperienced, new partner, John Vukovich, who, throughout the film, hovers between the partner governed by department codes and the buddy willing to bend them.

The filmic story is energized by its polarities. The most obvious polarity, Chance versus Masters, stages an encounter between one (Richard Chance) whose masculine identity is a result of pure chance: the arbrariness of birth and the present social practices of gender and sexuality, and one (Erik Masters) who controls his sexuality, inventing it very much the way he invents money. There is also a markedly black versus white polarity carried on within Los Angeles proper, as Masters visits a black neighbourhood to purchase a prison murder from his black buyer, who has connections within the Obispo penitentiary, where the hit is supposed to take place. Much is made of the sub-cultural partitions between the two separate criminal spheres, which are not unrelated to the more general economic separations between black and white society. For example, Masters offers $50,000 in counterfeit $100 notes for the prison hit on his 'mule' (arrested counterfeit deliveryman) whom he fears might 'roll over' in exchange for reduced time. But he is told that '$100s don't go well in this neighborhood.' The buyer wants $20s. There is an obvious entanglement between monetary and ethnic currencies.

Another major polarity is that between the bureaucratic police administration, whose rationalistic structure impedes the virtual vigilanteism of Chance's approach to the bust, and the rule-bending practices of criminal investigation in general. The rationalism of policing is constantly juxtaposed to the practices of Masters, the artist. For example, most of the action is punctuated by digital read-outs of the date and time on-screen, to signal the rationalistic structures of policing, but in one instance, the juxtaposition with Masters's artistry is signalled as the on-screen time and date are presented in script.

The primary polarity in the film foregrounds the problem of value in general and money in particular. Masters, an artist as well as counterfeiter, crafts his money; there is a long scene in which he makes the money with a variety of sophisticated pieces of reproduction equipment but also by hand mixing his paints. And he is shown hanging one of his finished paintings on an outside wall and then setting it on fire. In contrast with Masters's tendency towards the ritual expenditure of value, both with respect to his artistic and commercial endeavours – the money he 'makes' is constantly distributed (and in one instance also burned up) – is the policing of currency, the attempt to control its flow and to monitor its correct value.

The police department controls its flow within its investigative procedures as well as within the city. Its rules prevent large amounts to be used to set up suspects by making 'buys'. The polarity is thus reminiscent of the difference between Georges Bataille's version of political economy, which emphasizes expenditure and the ritual destruction of value, and the saving, hoarding and controlling that animates official versions of economy and structures the regulations governing policing procedures.[41]

Helping to articulate this value polarity throughout the film is a contrast in the discursive styles of Chance and his police colleagues and Masters. The saving, hoarding, and controlling of monetary value is reflected in the language of police work, in which metaphors of containment are the rule. Catching counterfeiters is called 'bagging', for example. And bureaucratic language dominates police interactions, for example the use of the 24-hour clock as the police chief refers to the time and date at which events have occurred and to the numbers and pages of the policing codes, which the chief evokes whenever officers request assignments or equipment.

In contrast, Masters continually speaks ironically. His language suspends rather than contains. For example, right after he and his accomplice shoot Chance's partner/buddy Jimmie Hart, Masters looks down at the body and says, 'you were in the wrong place at the wrong time, *buddy*', making it unclear whether he is using buddy as a casual remark or referring to the male bonding rituals through which police construct their masculinity in general and their extra-legal investigative procedures in particular. And, after Chance, disguised as a counterfeit buyer, Mr Jessup, delivers half of the buy payment, Masters says, 'I like your work, Mr Jessup', and then laughs. The 'work' could be the incredible work of deception in which Chance is engaged, the simple delivery of the money, on time and in the right amount, or the extraordinary risks and work of obtaining it (Chance and his partner kidnap a federal agent carrying the money).

The ironic language applied to identity is deepened in this episode, because Masters's female partner (and *her* female partner) are present during this initial payment, and when Chance/Jessup says 'Who are you?', Masters's partner responds, 'Who are you?' Placing a surcharge on this identity interrogation is the fact of a significant difference in the sexualities of Chance and Masters. Chance and his 'buddies' and informants are unambiguously heterosexual. They frequent men's sports bars or striptease clubs, and otherwise manifest a hyper-masculine behavioural style, while Masters hangs out in a night club that features androgynous artistic dance performances by an ensemble in which his partner dances. In a key scene, Masters seems to be kissing a male performer in the dressing room after the performance, but when the camera cuts to a different angle the 'man' become his female partner. (At this point the film has effectively enlisted the audience's perceptions in its ironic play.) Moreover, in keeping with his approach to value, Masters at one point presents a gift to his bisexual partner. He pulls a blanket off her lingerie-clad, female partner, sitting on a couch in his home, and leaves them to enjoy each other.

For Masters, the representational aspect of the sex, its reproduced performance, seems more important than erotic fulfilment or affirmation of his masculinity. In a scene in which he and his partner are making love, their eyes are on a video being made. In sharp contrast is the scene in which Chance has sexual intercourse with Ruth, his informant, who must participate because Chance can revoke her parole at any point. Force, containment, and raw bodily consumption, rather than boundary crossing and artistic creation, characterize Chance's sexuality. And a display of super-masculinity is central to Chance's performance, for it is filmed in a way that apes a male striptease; the bedroom becomes like the striptease venue in which Ruth works as a receptionist.[42]

Sexuality is certainly foregrounded in *LA*, and cinematic sexuality invites an erotically interested gaze. It makes sense, therefore, that Sharon Willis emphasizes the gaze in her treatment of the masculinity–social space relationships in the film. She notes, for example, that the lovemaking scene between Rick Chance and his informant 'renders the male body as spectacle' and that the lovemaking scene between Rick (Erik) Masters and his bisexual partner directs the gaze 'away from the current sexual scene to the image' playing on the video monitor the couple is watching.[43]

Yet the 'gaze', in the scene in which what appears to be two men kissing turns out to be a man kissing a woman, is disabled. The spectator – invited into one expectation and then located in another – experiences an ambiguity as a result of the deployment of different camera shots. Here, I suggest, the emphasis is not on directing the gaze but, in a Deleuzian sense, on engendering critical thought. Instead of a way of seeing, the film, directed by cinematic thought, through its assemblage of shots instead of the logic of the action associated with the chase of the counterfeiter, invites a perspective on different ways of *being*.[44] The film therefore goes well beyond dwelling on sexuality and the related dimensions of enjoyment associated with the gaze. It resists the restrictive economy of heterosexuality while, at the same time, exploring the metaphoric interplay between controls operating across the money–sex–power nexus.

Juxtapositions rather than angles of vision and contrasts rather than the action storyline are therefore central to how the film thinks. The contrasts between Masters and Chance are, accordingly, more important than the attempt of one to arrest the other, and they are sharpened as the action unfolds; they are underlined by the differences in motion. Chance is on a rampage, seeking to 'bag' his quarry, and, throughout the film, he is in motion: for example, chasing suspects on foot, and fleeing from the federal agent's 'cover' people in a long car chase. Masters is rarely shown in pursuit or flight. While Chance races across the city, mapping the different spaces in a blur of motion, Masters remains calm, engaging in ironic commentaries that blur boundaries: between hetero- and homosexuality, between racism and racial difference, between producing value and consuming it, and between policing and criminal activity.

Masters's suspensive irony governs the film allegorically until the end, when his death ends a variety of suspensions. The ironic stance discloses, by its radical contrast with policing, the interrelations among anxieties over gender and sexual identity, the policing of counterfeiting, and the mediation of power and authority, all of which emerged as interconnected in the discourse of the Indian servant, Angela, with which this analysis began.

Friedkin's *LA* explores the sex–money–power association extensively. The narrative opens with a presidential motorcade on the way to a hotel in LA where Reagan is to speak. Then his voice is heard, intoning that while death and taxes are inevitable, unfair taxes are not. Reagan's dispassionate articulations about money are immediately juxtaposed to a Middle Eastern zealot's words, as the anti-counterfeiting squad, on temporary secret service duty at the hotel, confronts a man claiming to be a 'martyr', who blows himself up while shouting 'death to Israel and America, and all the enemies of Islam'. Here, a comparison of saving and hoarding life to protect value versus achieving value by expending life passionately is presented as analogous to saving and hoarding versus spending money.

The rooftop hotel scene introduces us to the first pair of partners or 'buddies', which is about to be sundered, for Jimmie Hart is soon to retire. And subsequent scenes are devoted to the intense male bonding of the policing agents, focused especially on a retirement party for Hart in a hyper-masculine bar setting. The masculinity tropes are over-determined; for example, the young partner, Chance, is seen bridge-jumping with a bungee cord just before the party, and he mentions the thrill of having his 'balls in his throat'. This line operates on another register, for Chance's discourse is also hyper-masculine and never ironic. And his retirement gift to Hart is a collapsible fishing rod, which he delivers, mentioning that he must get rid of it because it is 'burning a hole in his truck'. The phallic aspect of the gift is underscored as Hart gives it a shake to make it extend.

Throughout the film, the male-bonding scenes are complemented by the exploration of various spaces of masculinity: bars and strip joints, which the police and their suborned accomplices frequent. More generally, the film explores social space in a way that exemplifies its various enclosures, not only highlighting spaces of masculinity but also ethnic neighbourhoods (for example, the black ghetto), artistic venues, police headquarters, prisons, and hospitals. But the film also makes clear what knits these various enclosures together. It focuses on a variety of complex exchanges within and between these venues.

In early scenes, money is shown changing hands, as men pay prostitutes, customers pay grocers, and buyers pay drug dealers. It is clear that counterfeit money is circulating in the ordinary exchange circuits of the city, and, at the same time, it is clear that flows of money cut across the partitioned ethnoscapes constituting the city. Other modes for transversing the enclosures are also an important part of the film's visual signification. The panning of the city scape dwells on conveyances, showing a train yard, a used car lot, oil rigs, and even a horse pulling a junk wagon.

Much of the filmic rhetoric is conducted through body shots. Chance struts and preens like a rooster, and his sexual and violent acrobatics suggest that the testosterone tank is always full. His pursuit of Masters, the counterfeiter, to avenge the death of his former partner, Hart, constitutes a model of (repressed) male fulfilment, a man chasing a man (as Judith Butler has noted, much of the impetus of male heterosexuality may well emerge from a frustrated homosexuality).[45] The fragile boundaries involved in male bonding and agonism – men with and against men – are thematized throughout. The most affectionate gesture Chance and Hart can evince is a punch in the arm, but when Chance makes a buy in disguise to entrap Masters, there is a groping scene. Masters presses up against Chance and pats his body all over, supposedly checking to see if he is armed. 'Are you packing?' he asks. And lest this ambiguous word play be missed, he adds, 'You're beautiful.'

Throughout the film, sexuality for Masters is accompanied by the play of language and visual representations. While Chance makes it clear that his sexuality is part of his control over money, his attempt to erase the counterfeit, Masters plays with boundaries. In addition to gifting his partner to her lesbian partner and showing a more general preoccupation with seeing rather than having, he plays with homoeroticism in a variety of ways. In addition to the *double entendres* he delivers while confronting Chance, his contention with his black counterfeit customer, who botched the in-prison murder for hire, is rife with homoeroticism. He sticks a gun barrel in the man's mouth, aping oral sex. Masters's articulations also abound in homoerotic imagery. For example, after killing a lawyer, Max Waxman, who swindled him, he says, 'Your taste is in your ass', as he turns a familiar disparagement about artistic taste (he is holding one of the lawyer's objets d'art) into a homoerotic trope.

In stark contrast, Chance's sexuality is part of policing. There is no irony in his representations (his balls are always in his throat). Making it clear that his sex with Ruth is an exchange related to capture and control, he responds to her request for more money as compensation with the line, 'If you want bread, fuck a baker.' Moreover, while Masters's attraction to his partner seems to be inspired by the ambiguities of her sexuality and their shared vocations of artistic representation, Chance's subservient accomplice, Ruth, underscores the fact that pure masculinity is at stake for Chance, saying at one point, 'If you really had balls, you'd jump off that bridge,' as she points to a high one in the distance.

The entanglements between bills and balls as signs are deeply encoded throughout the film. Chance gets kicked in the balls as his prisoner – Masters's 'mule' who delivers counterfeit money – escapes. Max Waxman, the lawyer who steals from Masters, gets shot in the balls, and all the police pursuers worry about having enough balls. Moreover, having balls is closely connected to the policing of homoeroticism. At one point, Chance attempts to get a judge to release the 'mule', from prison to his custody. At first he gets an outright refusal. But when he says that the judge would cave into other authorities and resorts to homoerotic imagery, saying he would be 'spread-eagled on his desk for his asshole buddies', the judge shows considerable peek and complies with Chance's request.

The tale of the bills operates on both sides of the police–criminal divide. While Masters is oriented towards dispersal or distribution, he must nevertheless protect that distribution. Hence, after he passes $75,000 in counterfeit money to his black buyer, in exchange for the (subsequently botched) prison hit, he tries to retrieve it. The paper trial constitutes a dangerous extension of his identity. And he underscores the problem of an extension into an alien ethnic space. What he ultimately retrieves, he burns, and when his female partner asks why, he says it is no good once these people have had their hands on it. As is the case with all his discourse, the remark is another suspensive irony; it mimics a racist disparagement as it refers to an uncontrolled extension of Masters's vulnerability to arrest. It is ambiguous as to whether he is being cautious, racist, or both.

While Masters is often violent (always on occasions in which his money is out of his control), his relationship to difference is more representational than violent. This is underscored by the assemblage of camera shots when he shows up to retrieve his money from his black buyer. When the buyer returns home shortly after the prison hit is botched, the camera follows his eye to a white hand, that of Masters, visible from the doorway. Whiteness in the black area is shown as both a consequence of the movement of money and as a difference that marks what is peculiar about spatial segregation; living space is separate, but in various ways the separation enables structures of significant exchange, not only between black and white and policing and criminal milieux, but more pervasively throughout the social orders. And this irony is displayed with an aesthetic rather than violent trope when the storyline is following Masters (the Master ironist). The hand that crafts the bills is there to retrieve them.

Chance's attempts at retrieval – for example his escaped prisoner, the men he apprehends for credit-card fraud, and the courier he robs to obtain 'buy money' – are always violent and unsubtle. He utters disparagements not ironies as he takes down violators, accomplices, or recalcitrant policing cohorts. But his pursuit of 'bad money' contains a massive structural irony. The hierarchical structure of the policing of counterfeit money is irrationally stingy. The policing bureaucracy tightly controls buy money, so much so that Chance cannot get enough officially issued to set up Masters for an arrest (just as hyper-masculinity cannot obtain enough of an official warrant). Hence, after learning from Ruth about a courier with $50,000 (who turns out to be a federal agent, who gets killed in a crossfire), Chance and Vukovich – at this point a fearful and unwilling 'buddy' – rob him to get good money in order to chase bad money.

At a simple level, policing turns out to be at least as violent as the criminal behavior surrounding counterfeiting, but the contention within the police ranks seems to be as much involved with policing male homosociality as protecting the value of money and thus the more general social circuit of exchange. Good money and unalloyed maleness turn out to be equivalent. Men affirm their manliness for each other; that is a prime circuit of exchange, and throughout the film, the new partner, John Vukovich, seems unable to live up to the level of homosociality that Chance had achieved with his former partner, Jimmie Hart.

What Vukovich must do to begin to live up to Chance's model of a partner is to accept the rule bending and improvisation that characterizes Chance's quest to sacralize the male bond with his former partner by 'bagging' Masters. Vukovich is continually caught between his commitment to police procedures – as a son of a former officer, the rules represent a patrimony – and his desire to be recognized as a full partner by Chance. Ultimately, to be the right kind of policeman, he must disavow the authority of the state, represented by the confining bureaucratic rules of the department, expressed among other ways by the nitpicking complaint of the bureau chief that his ashtrays keep disappearing. These penurious preoccupations seem to engage the chief's attention more than apprehending counterfeiters.

Metaphorically, therefore, the state stands in the way of the consummation of the homosocial bond. Although it licenses the policing of counterfeit money, it quarantines its agents within a counterfeit male identity because of its hoarding–saving–constraining approach to currency. Ultimately, although fearful that he may be busted for collaborating in the kidnapping, robbing, and killing of the federal agent, Vukovich, after consulting the same lawyer that Masters employs, Grimes, decides that he cannot roll over on his partner and 'testify' (another 'balls' metaphor) against him. But, ironically, it is Masters who seems to provide the pedagogy through which Vukovich's ambivalence is resolved.

As Chance and Vukovich try to arrest Masters during the final buy of the counterfeit money, Chance is killed in a shootout, and Masters flees. Vukovich pursues Masters, finding him in his warehouse, and, in a final struggle, Masters ends up being ignited by a gasoline fire that he tried to use to kill Vukovich. We see Vukovich staring into a fire in which Masters's life – like many of his other artistic works – is consumed (in the end Masters's had not only made his life a work of art, he had it consumed like his works). Seemingly, the ritual destruction of Masters by fire, transforms Vukovich, for in the last scene, he demands entry to Ruth's flat. His gate and bodily demeanor are now hyper-masculine (much like his late partner Chance), and his approach to policing is now also like Chance's. When Ruth says she is leaving, Vukovich tells her that she is staying, and that she now works for him.

The end of Masters has produced in Vukovich an end of ambivalence. Masters's the Master ironist, who operated on the boundaries of monetary value, language, and sexual identity, is gone. As a result, Vukovich has crossed definitively over to the side of improvisational policing, operating by Chance's methods of blackmail and extortion. Similarly, Masters's former partner seems to end her boundary ambivalence as well, once Masters is gone. After collecting the video tapes of her sex scenes with Masters, she gets into Masters's car with her lesbian partner. She is left with only one side of her sexuality.

Conclusion: Absent Presences

Although at least two characters have seemed to move towards resolution, the film as a whole does not. What it treats is a complex of forces, a 'sex–money–power nexus' as Seizer described it. This nexus operates at the centre of contemporary white male angst and rage against the state. Various identity pressures provoked by technologies and changes in the cast of national characters, as women, ethnic groups, minorities, gays and lesbians achieve increasing recognition from official and cultural institutions and media, have made it difficult for the white male without significant status markers to affirm his value. Although there are many contingencies affecting how men respond to changes in structures of affirmation, the response of some, best viewed as a politics of *ressentiment*, a retreat to enclosures and exclusions, along with aggressivity and rituals of identity purification, has elevated anti-immigrant and, anti-gay and lesbian policy to prominence.

However, these political episodes in the United States are merely exemplary of a more general aspect of nationalism, one that seeks to impose strictures on the range of individual bodies that can be accommodated within an aggressive, hyper-masculine version of the national body. To conclude, I want to explore the state body–individual body more extensively in *LA* and then in some films that, in varying degrees, treat critically, relationships between individual bodies and the state in other national contexts.

In mapping the various connections between states and bodies, I have argued that the state is often an absent presence in interpersonal exchanges taking place at various levels of the social body. While, for example, *LA* focuses primarily on two male bodies engaged in a struggle within the boundaries of Los Angeles, the state makes an appearance obliquely. Officially, it is present because the policing of monetary value in general and the prevention of counterfeiting more specifically is a federal function. And while federal jurisdiction sets up part of the official context for the action, partisan politics at the national level enters as well through the voice of President Ronald Reagan, articulating the traditional Republican Party's defence of economic privilege with an attack on the taxing authority of government.

The warranting of monetary value by the state becomes confounded with the struggle to maintain the value of homosocial bonds early in the film, for Reagan's speech is in the background when the events precipitating the end of Rick Chance's buddy relationship with his long-time partner take place. Thereafter, there is an implied connection between a state in a process of remasculinization and the hyper-masculine sexuality driving Chance's pursuit of the counterfeiter. Masters is a quarry who is, at once, a target of vengeance because he is a lawbreaker who has murdered Chance's partner, and a threat to be eliminated because he ambiguates the boundary between true and false money, commercial versus ritual artistic products and hetero- versus homo- and bisexuality. To appreciate how the film connects these registers of authenticity with the power of the state, one needs to pay attention to the articulation of filmic space with the various spaces involved in the development of the narrative.

My analysis of the film thus far has emphasized cinematic time more than space. The emphasis has been on how the direction of the action sequences imposes a temporality that allows for a critical political perspective on the various relationships in the film. The assemblage of shots creates a sequence that resists restriction to the projects undertaken by the actors themselves, for example, Chance's drive to arrest Masters and Vukovich's to achieve a mature policeman's identity. However, the articulations between filmic space and the specific spaces of the city, addressed in the story that appears within the camera's frame, must also be treated to assess effectively the money–sex–power issues organizing this analysis.

While the space of encounter between the aggressive white male, Chance, who seeks to impose strict boundaries around money, gender and sexuality and the violent but ironic Masters, who ambiguates these boundaries, is always within the frame, the more general space of the film includes what is implied but exists as a context off screen. The story proceeds in what Noel Burch has identified as two kinds of filmic space, 'that included within the frame and that outside the frame'.[46] The state's role in this story is represented primarily by its printed currency, and in the guise of a federal agent who is part of the plot. But much of its role operates through the off-screen imaginary it supplies as a warranting foundation for maleness as well as for its money. Indeed, as an imaginary, it is *necessarily* always off screen despite its pervasive symbolic presence.

Filmic spatiality, therefore, provides an effective representative of the complex relationship of national imaginaries to interpersonal relationships, precisely because of its ability to connect symbolic forms to interpersonal actions. To explore the state–person–sexuality interrelationships that film can treat, therefore, it is propitious to consider films produced in other states in order to show how these connections are articulated in other national contexts.

For example, the two different cinematic spaces – one within and one outside the frame – function effectively to locate an interpersonal sexuality issue within a national context in Cuban director Gutierrez Alea's *Strawberry and Chocolate*, a story about how sexuality operates within a state that is constitutively homophobic. Under Castro, Cuba became a state 'preoccupied with intensifying the criminalization of homosexuality'.[47] And this juridical policing of sexuality took place in an already-prepared national/cultural context inasmuch as the founding Cuban national myth contained 'homophobic compulsions' which had given rise to a normative level of regulation of gender performance;[48] masculine Cubanness has been historically understood in radical opposition to gayness.

Influenced by this dimension of its political culture, post-revolutionary Cuba has politicized homosexuality well beyond issues of individual conduct. The Cuban politics of sexuality has been extended to the symbolic connection between sexualized bodies and the national body. It is this connection that operates both within and outside the frames of Alea's *Strawberry and Chocolate*. Among other things, the film effectively conveys what Sanchez-Eppler has called the 'Stalinization of homophobia' in post-revolutionary Cuba. The relationship that develops between Diego, a gay Cuban writer, and David, a straight, sexually inexperienced but politically committed 'new Cuban man', requires surreptitiousness. The Cuban state, with its homophobic presence outside the frame, is present within the frame through continuous and invasive local levels of surveillance, like a neighbourhood watch representative that Diego and David must elude in their meetings.[49]

The divisions of the spatial field, which locate a politicized Cuba on the one hand (represented by David and his militantly homophobic roommate Miguel), and a closeted artistic community on the other hand (represented by Diego and his artistic associates) are reflected in the division of cinematic space. The Cuba of incarceration with its UMAP camps of imprisoned homosexuals is an absent presence. This is the Cuba existing off screen but involved nevertheless in influencing the exchanges that take place among the characters on screen.

Yet for all the implied critique of political oppression of the artistic community that the film conveys with its storyline, its shot sequences, especially the juxtapositions of within and trans-gender relationships and the explorations of living accommodations, seem only to amount to a plea for artistic tolerance, not, ultimately, for a loosening of Cuba's homophobic nationalism. Diego ends up emigrating because of artistic not sexuality-related oppression. And, in various ways, Diego's homosexuality seems to be tied – by the way the camera explores his spaces of performance – to a bourgeois decadence that the film seeks to impugn, in accord with official Cuban ideology. The film ultimately leaves the historical and structural reasons for official homophobia out of both the implied and framed picture. It figures political issues in terms of conflicts between individuals and backs away from the political issues operating in the interface between a homophobic national imaginary and the personal exchanges upon which that imaginary impinges.[50]

Stephan Elliot's 1994 film *The Adventures of Priscilla Queen of the Desert* (hereafter *Priscilla*) is also framed in relation to sexuality-related interpersonal exchanges in the context of a homophobic national imaginary. And, as in *Strawberry and Chocolate*, the state is present as an absent, framing imaginary. The story focuses on a troop of drag queens, travelling through the Australian outback to perform in venues with less sophisticated audiences than are found in their usual, Sydney performances. The outback crowds are more in tune with the hyper-masculinity model of gender that represents Australia's dominant founding mythology. But apart from a context provided by Australia's rural homophobia, *Priscilla* is a story of identity and space that can be effectively framed by a perspective that summons critical thought about the domain of the political. Specifically, it can be analyzed in terms of Deleuze and Guattari's concepts of nomadic versus sedentary identity practices and smooth versus striated space.

Transvestites are deterritorializing personages; they intervene in the symbolic relays between personhood and nationhood. As was noted in Chapter 3, the surveillance that reinforces the tight boundary controls of nationalism is frequently deployed on sexuality as well. Hence an intense commitment to gender boundaries articulates well with a surveillant policing of national territoriality (as is evident in Alea's *Strawberry and Chocolate*). In the case of *Priscilla*, the spatial odyssey through the desert adds an important dimension to the film's disruption of the personhood–nationhood connection. The symbolic nomadism of the drag queens functions within a space of encounter between a nomadic people, Aborigines, and the state-oriented Australian settlers.

The outback constitutes a place that is partially outside what

Deleuze and Guattari call the striated space of the state. Striated spaces are heavily coded with normative boundaries such that movement within them always produces a tightly controlled ascription of identity to those who enter and traverse them. Striating space, according to Deleuze and Guattari, is one of the fundamental tasks of the state, a function aimed at preventing nomadism.[51] This function operates both physically and symbolically. When they say that the state 'does not dissociate itself from a process of capture of flows of all kinds, populations, commodities or commerce, money or capital, etc.', they are referring not only to border patrols, toll booths, and revenue collection, they also mean the function of coding. The state is in effect a 'town surveyor' and it responds against everyone who tries to escape its coding operations by striating space.[52]

In contrast, 'smooth space' has no normative significance other than what is enacted by those who traverse it. One such space is the ocean, that chaotic domain, surrounding land masses, about which Kant was so wary. In a treatment of Caribbean literature and its deterritorializing impetus, Antonio Benitez-Rojo has constructed the Caribbean geography as distinctive with respect to the world's, state-oriented spaces. Referring to the Caribbean as a meta-archipelago, he sees its symbolism as disruptive of the strict, nation-state geography the world has inherited from the European model. The Caribbean archipelago, he argues, 'is a discontinuous conjunction [of] . . . empty spaces, unstrung voices, ligaments, sutures . . .' and it 'has the virtue of having neither a boundary nor a center'.[53] Departing from Kant and Hegel's philosophizing, which consolidates, conceptually the state model, Benitez-Rojo's Caribbean, with its 'vast collisions of races and cultures' represents 'world history's contingencies'.[54] The Caribbean peoples are the 'peoples of the sea: the culture of archipelagoes is not terrestrial, as are almost all cultures: it is fluvial and marine'.

Deserts, like oceans, qualify as 'smooth spaces'. Thus the drag queens, who inhabit 'Priscilla' (the name of their bus) during their odyssey through the outback, resist the territorial imperatives of state peoples as well as the subjectivity imperatives of unambiguously gendered people. Like the people of the sea, they traverse a smooth space, the desert. And like Deleuze and Guattari's nomads, who 'make the desert' no less than being made by it, they carry contingency into venues that have sought to reduce it. They disrupt certainties, for example the tight relationship between biology and gender, and bring a critical and ironic mode of thought to what is a traditional space of nationalism and homophobia. The desert is more than sand, it is a space of uncertainty and flux:

> The sand desert has not only oases, which are like fixed points, but also rhizomatic vegetation that is temporary and shifts location according to local rains, bringing changes in the direction of crossings.[55]

Significantly, while their performances of gender crossing, during their journey from Sydney to Alice Springs, produce either silence or hostility among the Euro-Australians, they find hospitality among a group of Aborigines, whom they encounter because they decide to take a short cut and depart from the marked route. Their encounter with Aborigines in the desert is an encounter between two groups who, in different ways, are nomads resisting the coding of the state.

Historically, the state-making Euro-Australians settlers treated frontiers as domains of capture: they named places in the process of settling them; they transformed space into place, making roads and marking out districts.[56] In contrast with the Euro-Australian place making, which consisted of incessant naming and boundary and enclosure creations, for Aborigines, the outback venues of their habitation always contained neutral spaces, reserved as domains of negotiation and cultural encounter. Every neutral space was regarded as 'a legitimate corridor of communication, a place of dialogue where differences could be negotiated'.[57]

The Aboriginal practice of space therefore sets the context in which the encounter between the nomadism of transvestism and the nomadism of Aborigines turns out to be sympathetic. The Aborigines whom the drag queens in *Priscilla* encounter in the smooth space of the desert join their performance rather than abjuring it. And the camera work produces a critical temporality. Although the camera follows the lavender-painted bus rather than supplying a montage to assemble disparate narratives, the drag queen-Aboriginal encounter, composed of various cuts that show the bemused attention of several of the Aborigines and some depth-of-focus shots that show their desert venue in the background, operates within a critical temporality that challenges modernity's time of the state. In particular, the depth of focus shots, which stage the encounter within a space that represents a history of settler-nomad encounter, achieve the critical effect of framing a region of time that includes the past within the present and accomplishes the critical effect that Deleuze has attributed to the time image.[58] We see an older form of nomadism functioning in a space that has never been subdued, greeting with evident delight, a newer form, which is enabled by its spatial odyssey in its resistance to the power of a masculinist state that normatively proscribes trans-gender practices and same-sex sexuality.

The encounter therefore effectively articulates the older oppression of nomadism with the homophobia of the present. Moreover, the drag performances during the desert odyssey play with uncertainty through parody. In so doing, they effectively oppose a politics that seeks to weld signs to stable referents. In general, then, strident nationalism, which would restrict the range of becomings, and homophobia share the desire for a tight correspondence between signs and referents, for an unwavering reality behind all appearances.

Practices and events that introduce contingency and uncertainty into language (such as irony), into national space (like immigration), into sexual identity (such as transvestism) and into monetary ex-changes (for example, the change from commodity to representational money)[59] evoke inhospitable responses from who seek stable, non-contingent warrants for enclosing territories and identities and who want the state to perform as a symbolic Fort Knox to warrant not only the value of representational currency but also signifying practices in general.

There are of course alternatives to the politics of identity behind the white male rampages described at the outset of this chapter as well as to the more enduring forms of identity enclosure associated with some aspects of nationalism and the politics of sexuality. Because, with their use of time images, they highlight the radical 'when' rather than the 'what' of value emergence, some contemporary films supply critical modes of thought. They enact a post-Kantian practice of critique that opens a way to a different kind of political apprehension. They help to create the conditions of possibility for a practice of thought that does more than merely chastize the rage that is expressed in the individual rampages in the films of the 1980s and exemplified in some of the group politics of the 1990s, as angry white men scorn immigrants, gays and lesbians, feminist politics, and the globalization of domestic economy. They point to the implications of embracing a politics of ambiguity and an acceptance of an ironic rather than essentialist approach to conceptual boundaries and identity issues. They imply that rather than appropriating nation-hood in order to warrant particular identities, and rather than constructing a fortress against difference outside while policing exchanges within, there is a way of thinking the political that would encourage a re-establishment of frontiers (understood as domains for negotiating identities and practices of space)[60] instead of reinforcing boundaries. It is a thinking in which encounters with difference provide occasions for self-reflection and negotiation rather than security procedures and in which identity spaces are continuously deterritorialized, that is, kept loosely configured and used as vantage points to anticipate encounters rather than to defend against them.[61] It is a thinking, finally, in which value emerges as *provisional*: as negotiated moments of mutual intelligibility among uncompleted selves, not as a characteristic of an essential subjectivity or of a range of objects to be discovered.

Notes

1. The expression 'finite history' is used by Jean-Luc Nancy to represent the characteristic of 'our time', in which history cannot have either a definitive past or an expected future attributed to it. Finite historical events cannot 'take place' because there is no pre-arranged space for them to occupy. They are happenings that make their place in time. See *The Birth to Presence*, trans. B. Holmes et al. (Stanford, CA: Stanford University Press, 1993), pp. 143–66.
2. Susan Seizer, 'Paradoxes of Visibility in the Field: Rites of Queer Passage in Anthropology', *Public Culture*, 8: (1995), p. 93.
3. Ibid., pp. 93–4.
4. This view is developed by a variety of thinkers, but perhaps the most compelling elaboration is by Jacques Derrida, 'White Mythology: Metaphor in the Text of Philosophy', in *Margins of Philosophy*, trans. Alan Bass (Chicago: University of Chicago Press, 1982), pp. 207–72.
5. Alan Ryan, 'Elusive Liberalism', *New York Times Book Review* (7 July 1996), pp. 7–8.
6. A critique of Kant's emphasis on the 'thingness' of a value is provided by Heidegger, who notes, 'Kant has disregarded what is manifest (*das Offenbar*). He does not inquire into and determine in its own essence that which encounters us prior to objectification (*Vergegenstandlichung*) into an object of experience.' See Martin Heidegger, *What is a Thing?*, trans. W. B. Burton and Vera Deutsch (South Bend, Indiana: University of Notre Dame Press, 1967), p. 244.
7. Ibid., p. 8.
8. Friedrich Nietzsche, 'The Problem of Socrates', in *Twilight of the*

Idols, trans. Richard Polt (Indianapolis, Indiana: Hackett, 1997), p. 13.

9. Michel Foucault, *Discipline and Punish: The Birth of the Prison*, trans. Alan Sheridan (New York: Pantheon, 1977), p. 192.

10. See Foucault's remarks about the contrast between Nietzschean genealogy, which requires historical inquiry into the modalities of moral discourse, and simplistic (impatient) moralizing: Michel Foucault, 'Nietzsche, Genealogy, History', trans. Donald F. Bouchard and Sherry Simon. in Paul Rabinow (ed.), *The Foucault Reader* (New York: Pantheon, 1994), pp. 76–100. Treating the 'individual', Foucault does not ask about its value. Instead he notes that until well into the eighteenth century, heroes were written about while ordinary individuality 'remained below the threshold of description' in biographical genres. But, the emergence of disciplinary methods 'reversed this relation, lowered the threshold of describable individuality and made this description a means of control and a method of domination': Foucault, *Discipline and Punish*, p. 92.

11. As George Mosse has pointed out, modern nationalism has historically co-opted manly ideals. It is not surprising, therefore, that men's masculine self-recognition is closely tied to their felt affiliation with nationhood: George Mosse, *The Creation of Modern Masculinity* (New York: Oxford University Press, 1996), p. 77.

12. Susan Jeffords, *Hard Bodies: Hollywood Masculinity in the Reagan Years* (New Brunswick, NJ: Rutgers University Press, 1994), pp. 1–22.

13. Fred Pfeil, 'Sympathy for the Devils: Notes on Some White Guys in the Ridiculous Class War', *New Left Review*, no 213 (1995), p. 115.

14. Quoted from Tassie Gwilliam, 'Female Fraud: Counterfeit Maidenheads in the Eighteenth Century', *Journal of the History of Sexuality*, 6:4 (April, 1996), p. 518.

15. Ibid., p. 519.

16. Thomas Lacqueur has mapped this change in *Making Sex: Body and Gender from the Greeks to Freud* (Cambridge, MA: Harvard University Press, 1990).

17. Gwilliam, 'Female Fraud', p. 521.

18. Ibid., p. 547.

19. Jean-Joseph Goux, *Symbolic Economies*, trans. Jennifer Curtiss Gage (Ithaca, NY: Cornell University Press, 1990), p. 9.

20. There are many discussions of the performative aspects of identity. For a relevant elaboration of identity as performance, see Judith Butler, 'Performative Acts and Gender Constitution: An Essay in Phenomenology and Feminist Theory', in Sue-Ellen Case (ed.), *Performing Feminism: Feminist Critical Theory and Theater* (Baltimore: Johns Hopkins University Press, 1990).

21. Emerson offers this figure in *Nature*, where he notes that when he is 'in the woods . . . standing on the bare ground', where 'all mean egoism vanishes. I become a transparent eyeball; I am nothing'. See Donald McQuade (ed.), *Selected Writings of Emerson* (New York: Random House, 1981), p. 6.

22. Pfeil, 'Sympathy for the Devils', p. 117.

23. The expression belongs to Lindon Barrett, 'Exemplary Values: Value, Violence, and Others of Value', *Substance*, 67 (1992), p. 78.

24. Ibid., p. 79.

25. See Susan Faludi, 'The Naked Citadel', *New Yorker*, 5 September 1994. The Citadel's mentality is a vestige of, among other things, the territorial version of masculinity promoted by Theodore Roosevelt. As one commentator has noted, in his autobiographical writings, Roosevelt, an advocate of the production of an aggressive masculinity, 'fought to defend and create separate male territories where boys, male adolescents, and adult men could freely interact': Arnaldo Testi, 'The Gender of Reform Politics: Theodore Roosevelt and the Culture of Masculinity', *The Journal of American History*, 81: (1995), p. 1522.

26. Eve K. Sedgwick, *Between Men: English Literature and Male Homosocial Desire* (New York: Columbia University Press, 1995), p. 2.

27. Howard Horowitz, *By the Law of Nature: Form and Value in Nineteenth-Century America* (New York: Oxford University Press, 1991), pp. 8–9.

28. This discussion of govenance as a warranting power for extensions of the self is indebted to Allucquere Rosanne Stone, 'Split Subjects, Not Atoms: Or How I came to love: Or How I came to Love my Prosthesis', *Configurations* 1:, (1994), pp. 173–90.

29. See Mosse, *The Creation of Modern Masculinity*, and Mark Selzer, *Bodies and Machines* (New York: Routledge, 1992) for treatments of this period.

30. Stone, 'How I came to Love my Prosthesis', p. 175.

31. Georg Simmel, 'Money in Modern Culture', *Theory, Culture and Society*, 8 (1991), p. 18.

32. Much of my discussion of the novel and its historical context is indebted to Jean-Joseph Goux's treatment: *The Coiners of Language*, trans. Jennifer Curtiss Gage (Norman, Oklahoma: University of Oklahoma Press, 1994).

33. That Gide took pains to achieve an ironic distance from realist fiction is evident in his ruminations on the writer Édouard in *The Counterfeiters*. See Gide's 'Second Notebook', trans. Justin O'Brien, in *The Counterfeiters*, trans. Dorothy Bussey (New York: Alfred A. Knopf, 1927), p. 397.

34. Goux, *The Coiners of Language*, p. 21.

35. Ibid., p. 20.

36. Ibid., p. 23.

37. Ibid., p. 33.

38. This is described in Joel Dyer, *Harvest of Rage* (Boulder, CO: Westview, 1997).

39. Pat Robertson, *The New World Order* (Dallas: Word Publishing, 1991), p. 229.

40. See Goux, *The Coiners of Language*, p. 54.

41. Georges Bataille, *The Accursed Share*, vols I and II, trans. Robert Hurley (New York: Zone, 1988).

42. This aspect of the film is emphasized in Sharon Willis's excellent reading of it: 'Disputed Territories: Masculinity and Social Space', *Camera Obscura*, 19 (1989), pp. 5–23.

43. Ibid., p. 5.

44. My insights here have been aided by the discussion of Deleuze's emphasis on the ontological rather than the perceptual effects of cinema in Jon Beasley-Murray, 'Whatever Happened to Neo-Realism? – Bazin, Deleuze, and Tarkovsky's Long Take', *iris* 23 (Spring 1997), pp. 44–5.

45. Judith Butler, *Gender Trouble: Feminism and the Subversion of Identity* (New York: Routledge, 1990).

46. Noel Burch, 'Spatial and Temporal Articulations', in *Theory of Film Practice*, trans. Helen lane (New York: Praeger, 1973), p. 17.

47. Benigno Sanchez-Eppler, 'The Displacement of Cuban Homosexuality', in Michael J. Shapiro and Hayward R. Alker (eds), *Challenging Boundaries* (Minneapolis: University of Minnesota Press, 1996), p. 383.

48. Ibid., p. 384.

49. This point is developed in Paul Julian Smith's reading of *Strawberry and Chocolate* in his *Vision Machines* (London: Verso: 1996), pp. 81–98.

50. Here as above, I am aided in my reading by Paul Julian Smith's treatment, Ibid.

51. Deleuze and Guattari, *A Thousand Plateaus*, p. 385.

52. Ibid., p. 386.

53. Antonio Benitez-Rojo, 'The Repeating Island', in Gustavo Perez Firmat (ed.), *Do the Americas Have a Common Literature?* (Duhram, NC: Duke University Press, 1990), p. 86.

54. Ibid., p. 88.

55. Ibid., p. 382.

56. See Paul Carter 'Debatable Land', in *The Road to Botany Bay* (Chicago: University of Chicago Press, 1987), pp. 136–71.

57. Ibid., p. 165.

58. Deleuze, *Cinema 2*, p. 108.

59. The expression belong to John Maynard Keynes. See his *A Treatise of Money*, vol. I (London: Macmillan, 1930), p. 7.

60. Here I am influenced by William Cronon et al.'s discussion of the frontier period in the American west, referred to in Chapter 2. As I noted there, they employ the spatial model of the frontier to imply that the cultural confrontation involved a negotiation of relationships between the different groups. The relationship was fluid, non-institutionalized, precarious, and uncertain. Certainly there was considerable violence, but there was also a sense that co-existence required a resistance to fixity on both sides of the encounter. They go on to note that the frontier moment was quite brief; relationships ceased being invented in the process of confrontation as fluidity gave way to hierarchy, as the engines of state power and the interests they vehiculated turned the frontier or place of invention and negotiation into a series of regions, proprietary and juridical in structure and administrative rather than inventive in practice. Henceforth peoples, however different their interests, cultural practices, and inclinations were to meet on a space already marked out. See William Cronon, George Miles, and Jay Gitlin, 'Becoming West', in Cronon, Miles, and Gitlin (eds), *Under An Open Sky: Rethinking America's Western Past* (New York: W. W. Norton, 1992), pp. 3–27.

61. For a discussion that emphasizes this perspective, see William E. Connolly, 'Tocqueville, Territory, and Violence', in Michael J. Shapiro and Hayward Alker (eds), *Challenging Boundaries* (Minneapolis: University of Minnesota Press, 1996), pp. 141–64.

Index